Great
Literary
Friendships

Great
Literary
Friendships

JANET PHILLIPS

BODLEIAN
LIBRARY
PUBLISHING

First published in 2022 by the Bodleian Library
Broad Street, Oxford OX1 3BG
www.bodleianshop.co.uk

ISBN 978 1 85124 582 6

Publisher: Samuel Fanous
Managing Editor: Deborah Susman
Picture Editor: Leanda Shrimpton
Production Editor: Susie Foster
Cover design by Dot Little at the Bodleian Library
Designed and typeset by Lucy Morton of illuminati in 10½ on 15 Caslon
Printed and bound in China by C&C Offset Printing Co., Ltd.
on 120 gsm Chinese Baijin pure woodfree

British Library Catalogue in Publishing Data
A CIP record of this publication is available from the British Library

Contents

HEART TO HEART

ADVENTURE

HARD TIMES

Introduction

DURING THE CORONAVIRUS PANDEMIC which took hold in 2020 most of us, under various lockdown restrictions, were not able to meet our friends for several months, and during this time many of us turned to books, in particular the classics, for solace.

This should really come as no surprise, since throughout these much-loved and perennially popular works of fiction, close friendships abound. These are the intimate best friends of childhood, student days, romance, hard times or even a lifetime. They are entirely different from the social media networks of the twenty-first century; often it is just one companion who supports the hero or heroine on their journey through life's troubles and triumphs.

'I'll come with you', or variations to this effect, was the line which first inspired me to think about the role of friends in our favourite books. For me it captures the essence of friendship in times of overwhelming difficulties. It acknowledges that a friend can't solve things, can't always even give advice, but they can be present, and that in itself is invaluable. In various ways, Celia says it to Rosalind when she is suddenly evicted from her home; Sam says it to Frodo as he sets out for Mordor and what seems like certain death; Hermione says it to Harry, on many occasions, when all other arguments have failed; Tom says it to Huck when he reveals his fateful plan to hide out in a graveyard; Ratty says it to Mole when he is overcome by homesickness for his beloved burrow. Further back in time, Pylades, defenceless against the gods, nevertheless accompanies his friend Orestes on his terrible journey of vengeance, and in the Book of Ruth, Ruth insists on going with her mother-in-law Naomi to Bethlehem, whatever fate awaits her there.

Such valued companionship extends, of course, to happier times, and other life-changing events, including lending an ear when the hero or heroine has fallen in love. Many writers across the ages have had fun with this theme, creating long-suffering friends to become valued confidantes and comforters: Pandarus takes on this role in Chaucer's *Troilus and Criseyde*; Juliet's nurse and cousin Celia are among several examples in Shakespeare. On the darker side of romance, several friendships are tested to the limit when both fall in love with the same person: Jane Austen's Emma grapples with this unhappy situation, as do Maggie and Lucy in *The Mill on the Floss* and Lina and Elena in Ferrante's Neapolitan novels.

Once the seduction is over, however, it has to be said that literary friendships often falter in the face of marriage. Arthur Conan Doyle rashly has Watson propose to Mary Morstan in *The Sign of Four* and then spills much ink finding excuses for her absence until he eventually kills her off in time for Holmes's return.[1] Indeed, several of the duos in this book are the happy bachelors of Victorian and Edwardian times – Pip and Herbert, Mole and Ratty – able to have so much more fun than their female counterparts. Anne of Green Gables fears her friendship with Diana will end on the day of Diana's wedding, and it is true that their intense relationship recedes in the later books. In pre-twentieth-century literature it can be more difficult to find central female friendships that don't revolve around finding a husband, and male writers of previous centuries tend to see young unmarried women as rivals for male affection. Brilliant though it is, Oscar Wilde's witty portrayal of Gwendolen and Cecily – who, due to Algernon's deception, believe themselves engaged to the same man in *The Importance of Being Earnest* – nevertheless has its roots in this assumption:

> JACK ...Cecily and Gwendolen are perfectly certain to be extremely great friends. I'll bet you anything you like that half an hour after they have met, they will be calling each other sister.
>
> ALGERNON Women only do that when they have called each other a lot of other things first.[2]

But in the twentieth century, writers such as Alice Walker, Toni Morrison and Margaret Atwood embraced the role of the female friend: flawed, controversial, unreliable even, but ultimately free from patriarchal control. And, like her or loathe her, Bridget Jones ushered in a whole new genre of writing on young women and their pals which continues to resonate. Most recently, Candice Carty-Williams acknowledged her as in part an inspiration for her own successful 2019 novel *Queenie*, which she has described as the 'black Bridget'.[3]

Some intimate friendships, viewed from a twenty-first-century perspective, can now seem like suppressed same-sex relationships, cautiously described back when some such partnerships were criminalized. In Andrew Davies and Julian Brock's 2008 film adaptation of *Brideshead Revisited*, Charles Ryder and Sebastian Flyte have a sexualized relationship; and several retellings of the friendship between Achilles and Patroclus – of which there are many versions in classical literature – portray them as lovers. In Virginia Woolf's *Mrs Dalloway*, Clarissa remembers her friend Sally Seton with intense affection, savouring the moment when they kissed, which can only contrast positively with her conventional society marriage and hints at an alternative life, impossible for her at that time. Would Charles and Sebastian have been lovers if Waugh were writing their story now?

Whatever his sexuality, Charles Ryder is a character in the tradition of the 'bystander' friend, a man of modest means who becomes infatuated by a rich, charismatic, well-connected soulmate. He follows on from Nick Carraway in F. Scott Fitzgerald's *The Great Gatsby* and resonates in the characters of Richard Papen in *The Secret History* and Nick Guest in Alan Hollinghurst's *The Line of Beauty*. He is the intimate friend of a smarter set, longing to be accepted but always remaining an outsider. His narrative is often an elegy for a friendship that is now lost.

Other narrators look forward, hoping that the importance and meaning of their friendships will outlive them. Horatio survives to explain Prince Hamlet's actions to the incoming armies; in *Things Fall Apart*, Obierika defiantly honours his brave friend Okonkwo even in the face of retribution from the white colonists; and at the end of *The Lord of the Rings* Frodo imagines Sam reading to his children about their adventures from a big red book. In a more recent example, Elena's four-book narrative of her childhood in Naples and subsequent adult life (in Ferrante's Neapolitan quartet) is an urgent and compelling attempt to immortalize her best friend Lina.

The friendships in this book have been chosen from classic, mainly Anglo-American, bestsellers or books which, in one way or another, have proved influential on the portrayal of best friends in literature. I have avoided sibling relationships, though it must be said that they are often brilliant friends – Elizabeth and Jane Bennet, for example, or Margaret and Helen Schlegel in Forster's *Howards End*, or Scout and Jem Finch in Harper Lee's *To Kill a Mockingbird* – but I have allowed cousins since these have the more independent quality of having different sets of parents. The many friendships in mythology (such as Troilus and Pandarus, Achilles and Patroclus, Orestes and Pylades, Robin Hood and Little John, King Arthur and Sir Lancelot) are not included here, as their portrayals vary from source to source and are difficult to pin down in a definitive narrative. Finally, although there are many examples of friends who betray in the literary canon – Brutus in Shakespeare's *Julius Caesar* springs immediately to mind (his treachery famously exposed in Caesar's dying line, 'Et tu, Brute?') or Becky Sharp in *Vanity Fair*, Sandy in *The Prime of Miss Jean Brodie* or Toni Morrison's *Sula* – in the main I have preferred to focus on those whom we remember as true friends, remaining faithful to the best of their abilities.

Rereading these incredible books which demonstrate the power of human friendship provides a wonderful escape from the sometimes grim realities of everyday life, and some characters, so intricately drawn, seem also to provide companionship. Jane Eyre reaches beyond the page in her direct addresses to the reader; Helen Fielding has commented that 'the way readers relate to Bridget is perhaps rather similar to the way women relate to each other';[4] Don Quixote and Sancho Panza have become characters who entertain well beyond the bounds of Cervantes's novel. Organized into broad themes, the types of friends portrayed here echo across genres and centuries; you might find similar friendships in, for example, *Childhood* and *Adventure* or in *Romance* and *Hard Times*. Whatever the connection, I hope that these stories of unforgettable friendships will give cause for celebration of the friends who stay with us, in times of crisis and against all odds.

SPOILER ALERT Most entries include a description of the ending of the novel under discussion.

Childhood

A s WRITERS FOR CHILDREN know, in order to provide an adventurous and exciting narrative it helps to get rid of the parents. No wonder, then, that these poignant portrayals of friendships in childhood usually involve orphans or the loss of at least one parent: Jane Eyre is orphaned and her friend Helen has lost her mother; Anne of Green Gables started life in an orphanage; Tom has lost both his parents and Huck his mother; Anita's mother leaves the family home halfway through the book; Harry Potter is perhaps now the most famous fictional orphan of them all. But, as well as providing dramatic opportunities, the absence of parents also brings into focus the importance of friendships, such companions filling, or trying to fill, the gap left by a mother or father. Loneliness in childhood is especially hard to bear, and these iconic friendships provide much yearned-for comfort, be it an escape from the cupboard under the stairs, the fulfilment of a dream of an imaginary friend, a cast of quirky animals to bring companionship to an only child, or simply a kindred spirit with whom to test the boundaries of society.

Soulmates

HELEN & JANE

Jane Eyre by Charlotte Brontë

In this enduringly popular Gothic romance, Jane Eyre leaves
her cruel relatives at the age of ten to attend a boarding
school for orphaned girls. On turning eighteen, she becomes
a governess and falls in love with her employer, Edward
Rochester, only to discover that he is still married to his
deranged wife, who is locked up in the attic of Thornfield
Hall. Jane must endure homelessness, poverty and the
overtures of a religious fanatic before finding she is heir to
an unexpected fortune and being eventually reunited with
the now widowed Rochester.

At the age of eight CHARLOTTE BRONTË (1816–1855) joined her
elder sisters, Maria and Elizabeth, at the Clergy Daughters' School
at Cowan Bridge in Lancashire. Both Maria and Elizabeth became
seriously ill at the school and died of consumption within two months
of each other. When Charlotte published *Jane Eyre* in 1847 using
the pseudonym Currer Bell, Lowood School was recognized as a
fictionalized version of the Clergy Daughters' School by contemporary
readers. Charlotte modelled the character of Helen Burns on Maria

Brontë. When critics of the novel complained that Helen seemed too good to be true, she wrote defiantly to her publisher: 'she was real enough: I have exaggerated nothing there'.[1]

JANE EYRE is described as plain, pale and little throughout the novel. She is aware of her 'irregular features' and takes great care to be neat in her appearance. Rochester describes her 'light-footed running' and 'neat-handed alacrity'.[2] She has hazel-coloured hair and 'changeable' green eyes. But her childlike frame belies a steely determination and deep reserves of energy. Jane is pious without being zealous. As she reaches adulthood, she gains confidence in her own sense of morality, although her attitude towards Rochester's estranged wife betrays the prejudices of the time. It takes her fifteen years to be in a position to do so, but when she can she erects a tombstone on her friend Helen Burns's unmarked grave, bearing the word *Resurgam* ('I shall rise again').

HELEN BURNS is about four years older than Jane. Her home is on the Scottish Borders and she has been sent to Lowood because her mother is dead and her father is about to remarry. She has a thin face, pale and bloodless cheeks and sunken grey eyes, though her features are transformed when she is inspired by intellectual ideas. Helen describes herself as 'slatternly' and untidy; she is an independent thinker and doesn't like learning by rote, preferring instead to read books or daydream. Both Jane and the head teacher, Miss Temple, are drawn to her because of her intellect and her spirit: she is wise beyond her years; 'her spirit seemed hastening to live within a very brief span as much as many live during a protracted existence'.[3]

HELEN ON JANE

I read a sincere nature
in your ardent eyes and on
your clear front.

JANE ON HELEN
Helen, at all times and under all
circumstances, evinced for me a quiet and
faithful friendship, which ill-humour never
soured, nor irritation never troubled...

J ANE EYRE first encounters Helen Burns reading a book
in the gardens at Lowood School for orphaned girls. She
feels able to approach her because of the book, guessing that
a love of reading is something they will have in common. It
is no coincidence that the book is *Rasselas*, Samuel Johnson's
meditation on the search for happiness. Helen's stoicism,
philosophical outlook and belief in forgiveness help Jane to
learn how to be calm and rational in the face of hardship,
cruelty and injustice, all of which she will face in her early
years at the school.

When Jane first witnesses Helen's unjust punishments at
the hands of despised teacher Miss Scatcherd, she is infuriated
and filled with passionate indignation on behalf of her friend.
'If she struck me with that rod, I should get it from her hand;
I should break it under her nose', she tells Helen. But Helen's
answer is not what she expects to hear:

> 'Probably you would do nothing of the sort: but if you did,
> Mr. Brocklehurst would expel you from the school; that
> would be a great grief... It is far better to endure patiently
> a smart which nobody feels but yourself, than to commit
> a hasty action whose evil consequences will extend to all
> connected with you...'[4]

Helen's wise advice comes into play shortly afterwards when Jane herself is publicly accused by the school's patron of being a liar and forced to stand on a chair in front of all the pupils. Helen supports her friend not by arguing on her behalf – which would be futile – but by deliberately walking near to her and giving her a supportive smile: 'What a smile! I remember it now, and I know that it was the effluence of fine intellect, of true courage; it lit up her marked lineaments ... like a reflection from the aspect of an angel.'[5] Later, when Jane has been left in isolation, Helen brings her food and holds her hand in companionship. The advice she gives then informs Jane's actions and decisions throughout the course of the novel, when faced at various points with a cruel deception, a bigamous marriage, homelessness, poverty and disapproval: 'If all the world hated you, and believed you wicked, while your own conscience approved you, and absolved you from guilt, you would not be without friends.'[6]

While Jane learns how to get on at school and, following Helen's guidance, wins the approval of the head teacher, Miss Temple, Helen becomes more and more frail. Realizing very late in the day that her friend is dying (though this is indicated early on to the reader by her frequent coughing), Jane sneaks into her room at night to comfort Helen on her deathbed. She is only just in time. Jane is found by a servant in the morning, embracing her dead friend in her sleep.

Helen's death occurs in chapter 9 of the novel, with three-quarters of the story yet to come: a highly unconventional portrayal of a friendship. But her influence on Jane's character resonates through the story. She is explicitly described once more when Jane is called to her hateful aunt's deathbed at Gateshead, and it must be the thought of her 'well-remembered tones' and 'sublime gaze' that enables Jane to forgive her aunt and ask in turn for forgiveness for her temper as a young child.[7]

After Helen's death and Miss Temple's marriage, Jane once again has no one to turn to and there is a notable lack of friendship throughout the rest of the novel. Her cousins Georgiana and Eliza are more enemies than friends; Rosamond Oliver, her visitor at Morton, is not much more than a social climber; St John Rivers proves incapable of friendship after Jane turns down his offer of marriage; and his sisters, Diana and Mary, only really become proper friends when Jane can be honest with them about her relationship with Rochester, at the end of the novel.

Without anyone to confide in, at several points of crisis Jane has lengthy discussions with herself – often presented in dialogue – about what to do next: 'How do people do to get a new place? They apply to friends, I suppose: I have no friends.'[8] At Thornfield Hall, where she is governess, there is potential for friendship with the housekeeper, Mrs Fairfax, but she proves too old and vague, and in fact it is her employer, Rochester, who most often refers to Jane as his 'little friend', a way of indicating that their eventual relationship will be based on the equality of friendship (as well as fortune).

Jane also, famously, addresses the reader directly. This is, of course, a widespread convention in eighteenth- and nineteenth-century fiction. But here, writing in the first person, Brontë uses it to enable her character to describe to us, the readers, Jane's innermost feelings. In the absence of a best friend, the reader becomes her confidante, and perhaps this intimacy between character and reader is one of the reasons the novel continues to be loved by new generations: 'I have told you, reader, that I had learnt to love Mr. Rochester: I could not unlove him now', she confesses, when she fears Rochester's attraction to the beautiful Miss Ingram.[9] 'Reader, I forgave him at the moment and on the spot', she tells us, the day after the awful discovery of the estranged wife in the attic.[10] 'It is a fine thing, reader, to be lifted in a moment from indigence to wealth … but not a matter one can comprehend, or consequently enjoy, all at once',[11] she explains when St John has revealed her inheritance from her long-lost uncle. And she begins the closing chapter with the most famous line of all, 'Reader, I married him.' Ten years later, 'To be together is for us to be at once as free as in solitude, as gay as in company. We talk, I believe, all day long.' It is the now remorseful and repentant Rochester who, in the end, becomes her best friend.

Liberty and Conformity

TOM & HUCK, HUCK & JIM

The Adventures of Tom Sawyer &
The Adventures of Huckleberry Finn
by Mark Twain

Tom Sawyer and Huckleberry Finn live in the small town
of St Petersburg on the Mississippi River. They share a love
of midnight escapades, which puts them in real danger when
they witness an actual murder. Further adventures involve
running away to an island, searching for buried treasure,
outwitting conmen, faking their identities and rescuing Jim,
a runaway slave.

MARK TWAIN was the pen name of printer, riverman, journalist
and renowned author Samuel Langhorne Clemens (1835–1910). He
is famously referenced in Ernest Hemingway's memoir, *Green Hills
of Africa*: 'all modern American literature comes from one book by
Mark Twain called *Huckleberry Finn*'.[12] Twain's decision to write *The
Adventures of Huckleberry Finn* in Huck's vernacular voice was indeed
groundbreaking, and a departure from the third-person narrative of
The Adventures of Tom Sawyer (1876). Published in 1884 (1885 in the
USA) but set around forty years earlier, the story enabled him to
brilliantly satirize the hypocrisy and racism of society in the American
South. In striving for authentic representation of dialects, he included

racist insults, a decision which is the subject of ongoing debate among critics and educators. One publisher in the USA has edited the text to avoid the N-word, while the critic Sarah Churchwell has argued that this dilutes the point of the book: 'Huckleberry Finn starts out racist in a racist society, and stops being racist and leaves that society. These changes mean the book ceases to show the moral development of his character.'[13]

TOM SAWYER is an orphan who lives with his annoying brother Sid at his Aunt Polly's house. Aged about eleven or twelve in the first book, he loves adventure stories and leads his friends in elaborate games based on Robin Hood, pirates and *Don Quixote* (see p.125), in which he is the hero. He is deeply superstitious and interested in ghosts and witches. He finds school – which he often skips – tedious, but this is alleviated somewhat by his adoration of schoolmate Becky Thatcher. Tom is adept at trading schoolboy 'treasures' such as milk teeth, pinch bugs and ticks, and has a talent for climbing out of windows and hiding his misdemeanours. He loves to have an audience.

HUCKLEBERRY FINN is the same age as Tom Sawyer. He, too, has lost his mother, and his father is a drunkard who disappears for months at a time. Huck sleeps in doorways and empty hogsheads (barrels). The mothers of the town dislike him because he is 'idle and lawless and vulgar and bad – and because all their children admired him so…'[14] He is used to being wrongly accused and describes himself as 'low-down and ornery'.[15] He smokes, swears, doesn't wash and never goes to school or church, wears tattered men's clothes, and relies on fishing, stealing and the goodwill of the community for food. He prefers the woods and the river to 'cussed smothery houses'[16] and hates being the centre of attention.

JIM is a black slave owned by devout St Petersburg resident Miss Watson. He is a big man. Like both Tom and Huck, he is very knowledgeable about folklore and extremely superstitious: he owns a hairball removed from an ox's stomach, which he claims can tell fortunes, and he is always alert to bad omens. Sometimes these prove crucial, as when he predicts a storm and so keeps Huck safe on Jackson's Island. His wife is enslaved on a nearby farm with their two children, 'Lizabeth and Johnny. Jim escapes from Miss Watson's house when he overhears that she intends to sell him to a slave trader. Unfortunately for him this coincides with Huck's disappearance, so not only does he become a runaway but he is also wanted on suspicion of murder. Jim is handy at fixing up a raft and cooking and acquiring provisions. He has a fatherly affection for Huck: he protects him from seeing his pap's corpse and stays close even when Huck gets taken in by a white family.

> *What you want, above all things, on a*
> *raft, is for everybody to be satisfied, and*
> *feel right and kind towards the others.*

THE NAMES TOM Sawyer and Huckleberry Finn immediately conjure up a sense of quintessential boyhood adventure: sneaking out at night, running away to an island, finding buried treasure, making up secret signals and passwords. These boys know how to 'borrow' a boat, make a raft, imitate a cat, light a campfire, fish for their supper, swim across a river and steal a ham from a larder. What's more, they mostly also know how to get away with it. Twain's portrait of young boys and their irresistible 'spirit of adventure' has captured the heart of many a reader with nostalgic memories of the freedom of childhoods spent playing make-believe and exploring the outdoors. As they mature, however, their friendship takes a more complex and sinister turn.

In *The Adventures of Tom Sawyer*, narrated in the third person but mostly from Tom's point of view, Tom and Huck's friendship is firmly established. Tom is the cleverest of his peers and the leader of their games of make-believe battles, which he always wins, and Huck is the most mature, having had to fend for himself from an early age. They have an instinctive understanding of each other and a joint interest in superstitions and folk cures. In an early encounter, Huck can't resist swapping a tick he has captured for Tom's recently extracted tooth:

> 'Less see it.'
>   Tom got out a bit of paper and carefully unrolled it. Huckleberry viewed it wistfully. The temptation was very strong. At last he said:
>   'Is it genuwyne?'
>   Tom lifted his lip and showed the vacancy.
>   'Well, all right,' said Huckleberry, 'it's a trade.'[17]

Huck also has a dead cat, which piques Tom's interest and sets them off on a midnight adventure to the graveyard (where they intend to watch for devils by a recently dug grave and offer the cat in return for the corpse as a cure for warts). As a consequence of this, they witness a murder.

For all his 'letting on' about heroic deeds, Tom readily admits to his friend that he is scared in the graveyard at night, and they forget about bravado in order to comfort each other and think up ways to ward off the evil spirits. Instead of these, however, they come across three local men who appear to be intent on grave-robbing: Doctor Robinson, Muff Potter and so-called Injun Joe. When, after a scuffle, Joe plunges a knife into Doctor Robinson and sets up Muff Potter to take the blame, the boys flee at the first opportunity. Huck realizes the real danger they are in as witnesses and suggests they swear an oath to keep 'mum' and shake on it. Tom's 'whole being applauded this idea' and he makes it into an elaborate ritual that involves signing their initials in blood, as if they are in one of his make-believe games. But, even so, the real effect of witnessing the violence is the same on both, and as the trial approaches they seek each other out to relieve the burden of the secret and the awful knowledge that the wrong man will be convicted of murder.

Huck's instinct is to flee and fend for himself, and Tom's impulse is to look after him. This is endearing in the early episodes of *Tom Sawyer*. When the boys return from being 'outlaws' on Jackson's Island in order to attend their own funerals (the town has presumed them drowned), Tom, revelling in the affection and relief of his own family, is aghast that no one is there for his friend and he tells his aunt 'it ain't fair. Somebody's got to be glad to see Huck', exhorting her to lavish 'loving attentions' on him, despite his discomfort.[18] Later, when they are looking for buried treasure and fantasizing about what to do with it if they find any, Tom admits he wants to get married. Huck protests 'I'll be more lonesomer than ever', so Tom immediately invites him to live with him and his future wife.

Tom, though ready to rebel against his aunt's rules at the drop of a hat, is already starting to conform. Despite his oath to Huck, he does in the end make a witness statement to the court, which secures Muff Potter's release. His vision of the future includes getting married to Becky Thatcher. At the end of the book, he wants Huck to stick it out at the Widow Douglas's house (she has adopted him and undertaken to educate him, with the help of her sister, Miss Watson). Their exchange on this subject shows how children use group friendships to exercise arbitrary power (Anita in *Anita and Me*, p. 37, is a fine example of this) and prefigures the deeper satire of Twain's later book, *The Adventures of Huckleberry Finn*:

> 'But Huck, we can't let you into the gang if you ain't respectable, you know.'
>
> Huck's joy was quenched.
>
> 'Can't let me in, Tom? Didn't you let me go for a pirate?'
>
> 'Yes, but that's different. A robber is more high-toned than what a pirate is – as a general thing. In most countries they're awful high up in the nobility – dukes and such.'
>
> 'Now, Tom, hain't you always ben friendly to me? You wouldn't shet me out, would you, Tom? You wouldn't do that, now, *would* you, Tom?'
>
> 'Huck, I wouldn't want to, and I *don't* want to – but what would people say? Why, they'd say, "Mph! Tom Sawyer's Gang! pretty low characters in it!" They'd mean you, Huck. You wouldn't like that, and I wouldn't.'[19]

Ludicrous ideas of propriety, ritual, race and what society deems right and wrong puzzle Huck many times, as in *Huckleberry Finn* he escapes from his drunk and violent father and embarks on his own adventures, heading down the Mississippi River on a raft with the runaway slave Jim. Twain's ingenious technique of having Huck narrate this later book in the first person enables him, through Huck's naive and uneducated commentary, to make a biting satire about the hypocrisy of a society that encourages feuds even though everyone has forgotten the reason behind them, follows a ritual or code only because it is deemed 'right', and, most of all, buys and sells human beings but champions freedom at the same time. Huck constantly thinks he is bad and immoral because his natural humanity in wanting to help Jim and the 'rapscallions' they encounter puts him in opposition to society's rules again and again, forcing him to lie and cheat in order to keep Jim safe. Although Tom is absent from the main part of the narrative, and in fact Huck has left his gang because he 'couldn't see no profit' in the elaborate make-believe, Huck harks back to him often – 'I did wish Tom Sawyer was there' – aware of his lack of education and therefore lacking confidence in his own ability to devise plans and schemes (the irony being that Jim quickly proves a much more sensible and reliable friend than Tom, and that Huck is managing very well on his own).[20]

Though Huck initially plays tricks on Jim and compares him unfavourably to Tom, especially when trying to persuade him to do something risky, he soon realizes that Jim is 'most always right' and appreciates his companionship and his protection in keeping watch at night. He is taken aback by the power of Jim's emotions when they find each other again after being separated by thick fog, each assuming the other drowned – 'my heart wuz mos' broke bekase you wuz los', en I didn' k'yer no' mo' what become er me...'[21] When Jim is recaptured, it is the memory of their friendship which steers him away from writing to Miss

Watson to tell her where her 'property' can be found, even though the rules of society dictate that this is what he should do. He recalls how Jim 'would always call me honey, and pet me and do everything he could think of for me ... and said I was the best friend old Jim ever had in the world'.[22] Huck tears up his letter even though he firmly believes he will go to hell for helping Jim to escape. He still believes they are on the wrong side of morality as well as the law when Tom Sawyer offers to help rescue Jim and confides that he 'fell considerable in my estimation' at this point.[23]

The satire reaches a farcical zenith in the much-debated last part of the book, in which Tom (pretending to be his brother, Sid), aided by Huck (pretending to be Tom), devises a ludicrously elaborate plan to break out the recaptured Jim from his flimsy and unguarded jail on Aunt Sally's plantation.[24] Tom here indulges in the ridiculously convoluted ideas of adventure stories by placing more and more obstacles in the way of Jim's otherwise relatively easy escape and bending everyone to his will: 'Tom superintended', says Huck, still believing in him at this stage. 'He could out-superintend any boy I ever see. He knowed how to do everything.'[25]

But when Tom admits that Jim is in fact already free – Miss Watson, now dead, has granted his freedom in her will – and Tom has known this all along, the scales finally fall from Huck's eyes. In the last chapter he challenges Tom about what his actual intentions had been, and Tom explains that he wanted the three of them to go on an adventure to the mouth of the river and then bring Jim back in style on a steamboat and 'waltz him into town with a torchlight procession and a brass-band, and then he would be a hero, and so would we'. Tom still sees Jim as a project – a means to improve his own standing in the world – whereas Huck has got to know him has a fellow human being, someone with whom to stargaze and laugh and chat around a campfire, whenever life on the raft allowed it, and someone who suffers from homesickness and the fear that he will never see his family again. He is therefore finally unimpressed with Tom – including his attempts to make things right by giving Jim 40 dollars – and his deadpan narrative says it all: 'I reckoned it was about as well the way it was.'[26]

Tom and Huck's friendship with Jim in this section of the book has drawn much debate and criticism. Why does Huck allow Tom to play these elaborate and cruel games with his friend's freedom, with such little resistance? One possible interpretation put forward by critics is that Twain was in part reflecting the fact that although slavery had been abolished for twenty years by the time he published the novel, the southern states were bringing in more and more rules on racial segregation, so that freed slaves and their children gained liberty only to find that a new set of laws took it away from them.[27] The games Tom instigates can therefore be viewed as an allegory of the law-making happening as Twain was writing the book. For his part, Jim never ceases to trust 'ole true Huck' and even sacrifices his freedom again in order to get medical help when Tom is shot in the leg during the elaborate 'rescue', proving his moral superiority.

At the end of the story Tom's Aunt Polly arrives and the boys' game of mistaken identity is blown. The childhood chums will go their separate ways: Huck's need for freedom now irreconcilable with Tom's desire to be in charge of the rules at the top of the hierarchy, demonstrating the abuse of power by the state and the disregarded wisdom of its citizens. Tom will return to St Petersburg, where, as mentioned in *Tom Sawyer*, 'There were some that believed he would be President, yet, if he escaped hanging'.[28] Huckleberry, on the other hand, will continue to run from 'civilization' for the sake of liberty, whatever its hardships:

> I reckon I got to light out for the Territory ahead of the rest, because Aunt Sally she's going to adopt me and sivilize me, and I can't stand it. I been there before.[29]

Bosom Pals

ANNE *&* DIANA

Anne of Green Gables
by Lucy Maud Montgomery

A coming-of-age story about an impulsive and imaginative young orphan girl who is taken in by elderly siblings, Matthew and Marilla, and brought up in idyllic surroundings on Prince Edward Island (a province of Canada), this was followed by many further novels in the series, relating Anne's journey from girlhood to headteacher, then to her marriage to childhood foe Gilbert Blythe, and lastly motherhood.

LUCY MAUD MONTGOMERY (1874–1942) grew up on Prince Edward Island. Her mother died when she was just over a year old and her father sent her to live with her grandparents in Cavendish. She trained as a teacher and taught for several years before becoming a full-time writer. *Anne of Green Gables*, her first novel, was initially rejected by publishers, but on its eventual publication in 1908 it became a bestseller and has since sold over 50 million copies. It clearly draws on the author's childhood, although the village of Avonlea is fictional. Anne of Green Gables was swiftly followed by *Anne of Avonlea* (1909) and *Anne of the Island*, published in 1915 during the First World War. After the war, Montgomery contracted Spanish flu; though she survived, her best friend Frede Campbell MacFarlane died in the pandemic.

ANNE SHIRLEY is a skinny girl with long red hair, freckles and large pale grey/green eyes dominating a white face. She is an inch taller than Diana and their birthdays are one month apart. But her most captivating characteristic is her ability to talk with great enthusiasm about her likes, dislikes, hopes for the future and reactions to every new experience. She likes to have 'scope for the imagination', since her ability to escape into a fantasy world has enabled her to endure the grim reality of her early life as an orphan. When Marilla asks her about her upbringing, Anne says: 'What I *know* about myself isn't really worth telling… If you'll only let me tell you what I *imagine* about myself, you'll think it ever so much more interesting.'[30]

DIANA BARRY has dark curly hair, rosy cheeks, dimples like 'little dents in cream' and a merry countenance. Just as Anne wishes she could put on a few pounds to fill out her scrawny frame, so Diana wishes she could lose a few to avoid getting plump. Diana is skilled at dressmaking and sewing and has a good dose of common sense, even if she describes herself as 'a stupid little country girl'.[31] She is sometimes tactless but always well-meaning, and though she misses her pals when they go away she is never envious: 'Diana … possessed … the striking merit of an unselfish admiration of the gifts and graces of her friends.'[32]

ANNE ON DIANA
I solemnly swear to be faithful
to my bosom friend, Diana
Barry, as long as the sun
and moon shall endure.

DIANA ON ANNE
*I shall never love
anybody... any girl... half
as well as I love you.*

BEFORE she meets Diana, Anne Shirley has had several best friends, but they have all been imaginary. One was simply a reflection of herself with whom she used to chat, another was a particular echo which sounded in a long green valley in which she used to play, whom she named Violetta. Arriving in Avonlea for the first time, having travelled from the orphanage, Anne asks her guardian, Matthew, if there is a girl her age in the village. When she hears that there is a twelve-year-old called Diana in the house nearest to Green Gables, she is immediately predisposed to like her: 'What a perfectly lovely name!' The idea of being Diana's bosom pal is further encouraged by questioning Matthew's sister, Marilla. 'I've dreamed of meeting her all my life',[33] Anne enthuses, but Marilla warns Anne that she'll have to win over Diana's mother as well as Diana if the friendship is to thrive.

Anne doesn't get to meet Diana until chapter 12, about a third of the way through the first book in the series, by which time we as readers have become invested in her adventures. We've seen her quick temper, her sadness at the prospect of being sent away again (because Matthew and Marilla initially wanted a boy) and her bravery in the face of loneliness. By the

time the meeting is set up, we want it to work as much as Anne
does, and we share in her trepidation:

> 'Oh, Marilla, I'm frightened – now that it has come I'm
> actually frightened. What if she shouldn't like me! It would
> be the most tragical disappointment of my life.'[34]

But of course, shortly after being introduced, Anne and Diana
swear to be best friends forever (once the less imaginative Diana
has understood that swearing this kind of an oath is not rude),
with the passionate and solemn intensity that perhaps only
children of this age have (Tom Sawyer is similarly enthusiastic
for this kind of promise; see p.19). Diana is reading a book
when Anne first sees her, and Diana's mother is keen for her to
have a playmate her own age (her younger sister is only three)
to encourage her to go outdoors. Diana, in return, will teach
Anne songs, show her the places where beautiful flowers grow
and help her to make a playhouse.

Diana proves to be 'a very comfortable sort of a friend'[35]
and keeps faithfully quiet as Anne's exuberance causes her
to get into scrapes. She tells no one when Anne accidentally
dyes her hair green or her nose red in attempts to disguise
her red hair and freckles. She joins in enthusiastically with
Anne's imaginative games and adopts her romantic names for
the landmarks around them: Dryad's Bubble, Lover's Lane,
The Lake of Shining Waters, even if she herself, being more
practical, can't come up with ideas to match.

The first crisis in their friendship comes when Anne accidentally serves Diana currant wine instead of raspberry cordial, and

she stumbles home drunk. As Marilla predicted, though Diana immediately forgives Anne for her mistake, Diana's mother is furious and forbids them from seeing each other, allowing only a brief goodbye. Their parting is comically poignant:

'Ten minutes isn't very long to say an eternal farewell in,' said Anne tearfully. 'Oh, Diana, will you promise faithfully never to forget me…?'
   'I'll never have another bosom friend – I don't want to have. I couldn't love anybody as I love you.'[36]

But Anne soon redeems herself by saving the day when Diana's young sister is dangerously ill with croup, and henceforth their friendship is secure. They can see each other's bedroom windows through the trees and they work out a system of signals using candles and cardboard. They are free to roam the beautiful countryside and enact Anne's romantic imaginary games or simply enjoy each other's companionship and shared delight in their surroundings:

Anne, on her way to Orchard Slope, met Diana, bound for Green Gables, just where the mossy old log bridge spanned the brook below the Haunted Wood, and they sat down by the margin of the Dryad's Bubble, where tiny ferns were unrolling like curly-headed green pixy folk wakening up from a nap.[37]

Theirs is truly an idyllic childhood playground.

As they mature, Anne and Diana embark on different paths. Anne pursues further study and a teaching qualification; Diana becomes engaged to Fred (a farmer), and her ambition is to make thirty-seven doilies for her future marital home before the wedding day. Both struggle, at times, to accept that their lives are changing. Diana cries on the last day of school and worries that Anne will replace her with new friends at college. When she's away, Anne misses seeing the light from Diana's window through the gap in the trees, and they write to each other regularly. But when Diana gets engaged to Fred, Anne feels 'as if ... Diana had gone forward into a new world, shutting a gate behind her, leaving Anne on the outside'.[38] They have previously discussed becoming 'nice old maids' who live together for ever. What's more, Fred does not resemble the ideal man they have both dreamt up, who must be 'very tall and distinguished looking, with melancholy, inscrutable eyes, and a melting, sympathetic voice'.[39] Diana is first to learn to distinguish between fantasy and reality, and by returning frequently to the anchor of their friendship Anne eventually does too.

In Anne's eyes, Diana becomes inextricably bound up with the landscape she loves so much:

> 'Oh, Diana, it's so good to be back again. It's so good to see
> those pointed firs coming out against the pink sky – and
> that white orchard and the old Snow Queen ... And that tea
> rose... And it's *good* to see you again...'[40]

Anne and Diana also hark back frequently to the oath they swore when they first met and marvel at the fact that, despite their different journeys through life, they have never had a quarrel. When Anne worries that after Diana's marriage 'the old constant companionship could never be theirs again', Diana reassures her, on the morning of her wedding: 'We'll love each other just as much as ever. We've always kept that "oath" of friendship we swore long ago, haven't we?'[41]

For all Anne and Diana's romantic ideas, Montgomery doesn't pretend that moving away from Avonlea and having families of their own won't have an impact on their relationship, and references to Diana do recede dramatically in the later books. But the memory of their deeply founded childhood friendship lives on in the next generation: Diana names her daughter Anne Cordelia; Anne's twin girls are called Nan and Di Blythe.

Competitive Companions

WINNIE-THE-POOH & PIGLET

Winnie-the-Pooh & The House at Pooh Corner
by A.A. Milne

These stories recount the adventures, mishaps and milestones of an assortment of animals including Pooh, Piglet, Eeyore, Rabbit and Owl, and a young boy, Christopher Robin, who all live in the Hundred Acre Wood.

A.A. MILNE (1882–1956) based these stories (published in 1926 and 1928 respectively) around his only child, Christopher Robin Milne, and the stuffed toys Christopher played with at their family home near Ashdown Forest in Sussex. Milne was a playwright, novelist and essayist and reportedly disappointed that his fame as a writer rested on the books featuring Pooh Bear and friends. In his lifetime, around 7 million copies of the *Winnie-the-Pooh* books were sold: like *The Wind in the Willows*, the books enjoyed huge success in America. The original Pooh Bear and Piglet are now in the New York Public Library.

PIGLET is about the size of a birthday balloon and he lives in a beech tree next to a sign saying 'Trespassers W'. Haycorns are his favourite food. Piglet has had more education than Pooh because Christopher

Robin once took him to school in his pocket. He often has to remind Pooh that he is a Very Small Animal and that accounts for his general anxiety. He is easily embarrassed, and his 'excited ears' are often a good indication of his state of mind.

WINNIE-THE-POOH is about three times the size of Piglet – depending on how much honey he has eaten. He lives in a tree next to a sign that says 'Mr Sanders' and he is good at climbing. Although he is famously a Bear of Very Little Brain, Pooh's achievements are numerous: Discoverer of the North Pole, Composer and Poet, Finder of Eeyore's tail, Rescuer of Piglet during the great flood and Captain of The Floating Bear.

T HE FIRST CHAPTER of *Winnie-the-Pooh* opens with Pooh bumping down the stairs behind Christopher Robin, paw in hand, and the last chapter of *The House at Pooh Corner* ends in the enchanted forest where 'a little boy and his bear will always be playing'. But, although Christopher Robin clearly loves Pooh, and Pooh adores Christopher Robin, it is Pooh's relationship with Piglet that really encapsulates what a childhood friendship is all about.

Many of the adventures in *Winnie-the-Pooh* and *The House at Pooh Corner* begin with Pooh and Piglet calling for each other. They even have a 'Thoughtful Spot'[42] halfway between their two houses where they meet to decide what to do that day. They are comfortable enough with each other's company to walk together through the forest in a companionable silence, helping each other over stepping stones and holding on to each other when the wind is very strong. But they are equally happy duetting on Pooh's hums (the chorus of 'Tiddely-poms' memorably provided by Piglet during a very snowy walk to Eeyore's meadow). Piglet is no pushover, however. As all good friends do, he provides criticism where necessary, particularly in relation to Pooh's poems, songs and spelling, and though he lacks Pooh's confidence he is keen to match him, or even better him, in achieving success in the eyes of their friends. In doing so, he learns how to overcome fear in the course of the books.

In some ways, Piglet has the traits of a younger sibling who is trying to keep up. When he and Pooh are tracking a 'Woozle' and Pooh exclaims '*Look!*', Piglet jumps out of his skin and then tries to cover it up: 'to show that he hadn't been frightened he jumped up and down once or twice more in an exercising sort of way.'[43] When Christopher Robin mentions that he has seen a Heffalump, Piglet pretends he has seen one too, and when Pooh decides to set a trap to catch one, Piglet wishes he had thought of this first. He and Pooh argue over whose favourite food to put into the trap (until Piglet realizes the advantages of having Pooh supply the honey, rather than depleting his own store of haycorns). Piglet is also immensely proud to be described as 'useful' by Rabbit during one of his ridiculous plans, but his ego is soon deflated:

> 'What about me?' said Pooh sadly. 'I suppose *I* shan't be useful?'
>
> 'Never mind, Pooh,' said Piglet comfortingly. 'Another time perhaps.'
>
> 'Without Pooh,' said Rabbit … 'the adventure would be impossible.'
>
> 'Oh!' said Piglet, and tried not to look disappointed.[44]

Piglet races to give a birthday present to Eeyore because he wants to beat Pooh to it, which is partly why he falls down and bursts the balloon. But when the gifts are given (an empty jar of honey from Pooh, who had felt peckish en route) they seem to symbolize the synchronicity of Pooh and Piglet's friendship. The deflated balloon fits perfectly inside the empty honey jar – put together the gifts are transformed into something that works – and Eeyore takes great pleasure in placing the one inside the other and taking it out again, thanking both friends equally.

Pooh is the optimist and Piglet is the pessimist in this relationship. 'Supposing a tree fell down?' asks Piglet anxiously on a particularly blustery walk. 'Supposing it didn't' is Pooh's reply.[45] Piglet, however, is cleverer than Pooh, and Pooh in turn relies on this quality in his friend. When Rabbit orders him to join the search for Small, Pooh decides to 'begin the hunt by looking for Piglet, and asking him what they were looking for before he looked for it'.[46] Unlike Pooh, whose spelling is wobbly, Piglet can write his own name, which means he can send a message calling for help when he is cut off by the great flood. It is in this situation, stuck in his tree house after many days of rain, that, forgetting all rivalry, he so wonderfully summarizes the precious companionship that friends give:

'If only,' he thought, as he looked out of the window,
'I had been in Pooh's house, or Christopher Robin's house,
or Rabbit's house when it began to rain, then I should
have had Company all this time, instead of being here all
alone, with nothing to do except wonder when it will stop.'

And he imagined himself with Pooh, saying, 'Did you ever see such rain, Pooh?' and Pooh saying, 'Isn't it *awful*, Piglet?' and Piglet saying, 'I wonder how it is over Christopher Robin's way,' and Pooh saying, 'I should think poor old Rabbit is about flooded out by this time.' It would have been jolly to talk like this, and really, it wasn't much good having anything exciting like floods, if you couldn't share them with somebody....

And then he gave a very long sigh and said, 'I wish Pooh were here. It's so much more friendly with two.'[47]

Mad Bad Girls

MEENA *&* ANITA

Anita and Me by Meera Syal

Meena Kumar befriends Anita Rutter in the former mining village of Tollington in the West Midlands, in the 1970s. Intoxicated by Anita's disregard for authority, Meena believes she will now finally fit in with the village kids. But the National Front is on the rise and latent hostilities soon surface in their small community.

MEERA SYAL had already gained success as an actor and scriptwriter (she wrote the screenplay for *Bhaji on the Beach*, 1993) by the time *Anita and Me*, her first novel, was published in 1996. Syal's parents came to the UK from India in the 1960s and she grew up in the ex-mining village of Essington in the West Midlands. Although her setting of Tollington is fictional, she has explained that the novel is semi-autobiographical. *Anita and Me* was made into a film in 2002, in which Syal plays Auntie Shaila, and was adapted for the stage in 2015. The novel is now on the GCSE curriculum in the UK.

MEENA KUMAR is nine at the start of the story and a very wise eleven by the end. Her parents are both from the Punjab, having met in Delhi and moved to England to escape persecution following Partition. Hers is the only non-white family in Tollington. Meena wears T-bar sandals and frilly dresses or salwar kameez for special occasions. She is naturally rebellious and not afraid to use her fists. Lies come easily to her. Her sense of humour and extrovert nature win her over to many in the community, including Sam Lowbridge, who describes her as 'the best wench in Tollington'.[48]

ANITA RUTTER is about thirteen, already at secondary school and confident of her attraction to the opposite sex. She has green eyes, blonde hair, pale skin and a brown birthmark under one eye that throbs when she is angry. Anita likes to lasso younger kids with her skipping rope; Meena describes her as having 'the face of a pissed-off cherub'. She is as fearless as a Rottweiler and an official Bad Influence according to the mothers of Tollington. Anita's mum, Deirdre, takes little interest in her, and her father, Roberto, is abusive. Her friends are Sherrie and Fat Sally.

T HOUGH written from a very different perspective, in some ways this finely drawn *Bildungsroman* confronts a similar question to E.M. Forster's at the start of *A Passage to India*, when Dr Aziz's friends Mahmoud Ali and Hamidullah discuss 'whether or no it is possible to be friends with an Englishman' in 1920s' India under British rule.[49]

Here, though, we are in a West Midlands village in 1970s' Britain, and at the start of the book British-born nine-year-old Meena Kumar believes anything will be possible if only she can make friends with a big girl and escape from her ignorant classmates, her Indian parents' disappointment and the 'cloud of toddlers' who follow her around in her neighbourhood.

Anita Rutter fits this brief. Older, cockier, louder, one of the first things she says to Meena is a blatant lie: a claim that the sailor in the advert displayed in the village shop for Player's Capstan cigarettes is her father. On the day that Anita properly notices Meena for the first time and invites her to tag along, Meena herself has also been caught out in a lie and is awaiting punishment for having stolen money from her mother's purse. Anita represents something new and different: an escape from parental scrutiny, an absence of judgement. It's an important moment for Meena and she remembers it vividly:

> Because today, everything was fuzzy and unformed except for Anita, what she looked like, what she did, the way she made me feel, taller and sharper and ready to try anything.[50]

Their friendship is based on thrill-seeking: screaming down alleyways, trespassing in the grounds of the big house, stealing the charity box from the village shop, going on all the scariest rides when the fair comes and clinging onto each other for dear life on the Wall of Death. Meena has never had anyone with whom to do all these things before and Syal captures perfectly the intensity of this kind of whirlwind friendship, dangerously addictive, misunderstood and hyperreal.

But it comes at a cost. The festival of Diwali coincides with the fair, and Meena abandons her family's Diwali celebration to go to it. Inexorably, she starts wanting to shed her Indian heritage. After a day with Anita she asks for fish fingers and chips for tea instead of dahl and rice. After reading Anita's *Jackie* magazines, she wants to lighten her skin with foundation.

She adopts the West Midlands lingo with alacrity. Anita is her 'passport to acceptance' in the white working-class village of Tollington.

And, though Anita never takes much interest in Meena's Indian heritage, they do share a fundamental feeling of alienation. Anita's abusive father and negligent mother prompt her to become 'cock of the yard', the leader of gangs, in order to guarantee she won't be abandoned by her friends as well as her family. Meena's mother, meanwhile, gives birth to her brother Sunil and consequently has very little attention to give to Meena, whose struggle with identity is now becoming acute:

> I knew I was a freak of some kind, too mouthy, clumsy and scabby to be a real Indian girl, too Indian to be a real Tollington wench... And Anita never looked at me the way my adopted female cousins did; there was never fear or censure or recoil in those green, cool eyes, only the recognition of a kindred spirit, another mad bad girl trapped inside a superficially obedient body.[51]

From now on, the two girls call for each other every day, bump hips in their own special greeting, set up headquarters in an abandoned pigsty and make plans for the flat they want to share in London when they are older. Meena achieves what she thinks is total acceptance when she steals the charity box from the village shop in the presence of her law-abiding Indian cousins and earns a promotion from Anita:

> 'Yow'm a real Wench. That was bostin what yow did. Yow can be joint leader with me now if yow want, you know, of our gang.'[52]

Meena's father warns her, and the fortune-teller at the village fête also sees it, but it takes an excruciating public facedown for Meena to glimpse how illusory her feeling of acceptance really is. Local heart-throb Sam Lowbridge interrupts the annual fête with a racist outburst and gains support from some of the villagers. Meena feels as if someone has socked her in the stomach. Though she is standing next to Anita, she knows 'she would not hold me or take my hand'.[53] In fact, Anita describes Sam as 'bosting', oblivious to his speech's devastating effect on her best friend.

In this way Anita represents the subliminal racism of the community. Meena is surrounded by it, without it ever being specifically targeted at her. Even the sweet wrappers for Blackjack chews have a racist caricature on them, racist jokes at school go unpunished, some villagers have never bothered to learn her name, and the local mums always seem to focus on difference – in clothes, in food – no matter how much they enthuse over it. But Meena herself, unwilling to defy Anita, also participates in bullying, though she feels bad about it afterwards, observing how

> those you called friends could suddenly become tormentors,
> sniffing out a weakness or a difference, turning their own
> fear of ostracism into a weapon with which they could beat
> the victim away, afraid that being an outsider, an individual
> even, was somehow infectious.[54]

It is similar to the dangerous 'pack instinct' identified in himself and his friends by Richard in *The Secret History* (see p. 86), or the 'group-fright' experienced by Sandy, who simultaneously wants to leave and stay in her teacher Miss Brodie's exclusive clique (see p. 76).[55]

The arrival of Meena's grandmother, her Namina, coincides with Meena's first falling out with Anita, and brings home to her the richness and importance of her Indian heritage, something she cannot talk about to her white friends:

> Before Nanima arrived, this urge to reinvent myself
> … was driven purely by shame, the shame I felt when
> we 'did' India at school, and would leaf through tatty
> textbooks where the map of the world was an expanse
> of pink, where erect Victorian soldiers posed in grainy
> photographs, their feet astride flattened tigers, whilst men
> who looked like any one of my uncles, remained in the
> background holding trays or bending under the weight of
> impossible bundles.[56]

This growing knowledge, combined with the escalation of racism in the village (reflecting the rise of the National Front in the UK and the fallout from Enoch Powell's racist speech in Birmingham in 1968) prompts Meena to begin to question her own association with some of the village kids. She avoids Sam, but, on hearing that Anita's mother has left the family home, resumes her friendship with Anita, partly out of pity, but partly also for the chance to hang out at their friend Sherrie's farm and groom her new pony. It is here, with the girls she still tentatively counts as friends, that she learns of Anita's final betrayal. Anita is now Sam Lowbridge's girlfriend and has colluded in his violent racist attack on an Asian man. Unable to contain her feelings of anger and hurt, Meena's self-destructive reaction is to jump on the pony and ride it recklessly, culminating in an accident in which she badly breaks her leg.

Even though Meena makes a new, important friend in hospital (an intelligent, mature and sensitive boy named Robert) and resolves to spend her recovery time focusing on self-improvement and passing the eleven-plus so that she can go to a different school to Anita, she is still haunted by her betrayal. Initially, she can't stop thinking about Anita's reaction to the accident: 'she closed her face like the end of a chapter in a long epic book, a dying cadence, a full stop.'[57] Then she tries to erase her from her memory, consigning her to being Sam Lowbridge's girlfriend. She understands now, having thoroughly tested Anita's friendship, that being accepted by her racist gang would be worse than being ostracized by them.

If Forster's answer to his question, at the end of *A Passage to India*, is 'no, not yet...', Syal's is a more optimistic conclusion: there is still hope in Meena's family's move to a new bungalow elsewhere, the meaningfulness of her friendship with Robert and her place at grammar school at the end of the story. But perhaps the question itself is wrong: what is an Englishman? What is an Indian? No friendship can be based on reducing a person to a stereotype. This is something Samad Iqbal articulates to his white friend Archie Jones at the start of their long, troubled but enduring relationship in Zadie Smith's *White Teeth* (which appeared in print four years after *Anita and Me*):

'if ever you hear anyone speak of the East ... *hold your judgement*. If you are told "they are all this" or "they do this" or "their opinions are these", withhold your judgement until all the facts are upon you. Because that land they call "India" goes by a thousand names and is populated by millions, and if you think you have found two men the same amongst that multitude, then you are mistaken.'[58]

Meena's triumph is in understanding that she no longer needs or wants to conform with any strict idea of what is British or what is Indian: Anita has shown her that, and in doing so has made their friendship redundant.

Housemates

HARRY, HERMIONE & RON

The *Harry Potter* series by J.K. Rowling

Orphan Harry Potter is sent to wizard school at the age of eleven. There he must learn how to defeat Voldemort, the 'Dark Lord' who killed his parents and wants to become immortal in order to rule both the wizard world and the 'muggle' (non-magical) universe.

The *Harry Potter* series was published over a span of ten years, from 1997 to 2007. The first book, *Harry Potter and the Philosopher's Stone*, was rejected by several publishers before being signed up by Bloomsbury in the UK and Scholastic in the USA. To date, more than 500 million copies of the books have been sold throughout the world, and J.K. Rowling has become a household name. In an interview with schoolchildren, she confessed that her favourite characters are Harry, Ron, Hermione, Hagrid and Professor Lupin.[59]

HARRY POTTER is known by several sobriquets – 'The Chosen One', 'The Boy who Lived', 'Undesirable No. 1' – which go up and down in popularity throughout the series. He is notorious before he arrives at Hogwarts School of Witchcraft and Wizardry and amazed that this should be so, having spent his early childhood in the cupboard under the stairs at his 'muggle' uncle and aunt's house in Little Whinging. Fred Weasley describes Harry as a 'specky, scrawny, git',[60] and even his talking mirror despairs of his unruly hair. Harry looks like his father and has his mother's green eyes, though he remembers neither of them since he was only a baby when they were both killed by Voldemort. He wears round glasses and, most famously, has a scar shaped like a bolt of lightning on his forehead. He has inherited his father's skill at Quidditch and becomes the youngest ever seeker for the Gryffindor Quidditch team.

HERMIONE GRANGER is an only child whose parents are both dentists. She has bushy hair, rather large front teeth and a bossy manner. Hermione is always putting her hand up in class – she cannot resist the urge to answer questions. She reads avidly and her first port of call when in trouble is the Hogwarts library. But she is not just clever in a scholarly way – both boys also rely on her for emotional intelligence. ('You should write a book', Ron says, 'translating mad things girls do so boys can understand them'[61]) Hermione is very competitive in lessons. Harry says she has a 'mania for upholding rules',[62] but this only applies if the rules align with her own moral compass. When she decides to break them, there is no stopping her.

RON WEASLEY is the sixth boy in the Weasley family. He has a lanky frame, big hands and feet, a long nose, freckles and flaming red hair. When he is embarrassed his ears turn red. Ron has hand-me-down robes, wand and even pet: his rat, Scabbers, used to belong to older brother Percy. Ron is especially scared of spiders and he swears a lot. Nevertheless, he has the most experience of magic – having come from a long-standing wizarding family – and is the optimist among the three friends. Ron has the funniest lines, but he is not just there for comic effect: he is exceptionally good at chess, saves Harry from downing in an icy lake and turns out to be a decent keeper for Gryffindor Quidditch team.

IF YOU WERE LUCKY enough to turn eleven in 1997, it must have felt like you were growing up with Harry, Ron and Hermione, tracking their progress through the years at Hogwarts, which more or less mapped onto years 7–13 at secondary school. By the end of the series we know these characters intimately because we have witnessed their development, from eager and nervous eleven-year-olds to cocky twelve-year-olds, through awkward adolescence and finally to a maturity beyond their sixth-form years. It is a major feature of the series, and by developing not only the characters but also their relationships with each other over the seven books J.K. Rowling gives us a rich and complex portrait of friendships which turn out to be crucial to survival.

Like any school friends, Harry, Ron and Hermione certainly have their ups and downs. Harry and Ron are not at all sure about 'know-it-all' Hermione at first, but when she uncharacteristically lies to a teacher to get them out of trouble in *The Philosopher's Stone*, they begin to understand the value of her friendship. At times, Hermione mediates between Ron and Harry, particularly when Harry is chosen to take part in the Triwizard Tournament and Ron doesn't believe that he didn't put himself forward; and Harry often mediates between Ron and Hermione, who squabble a lot, especially when Hermione's cat Crookshanks seems bent on consuming Ron's rat. Later, in *The Order of the Phoenix*, Ron and Hermione tactfully ask a stressed-out Harry to stop taking his bad mood out on them. But their ability to get over jealousy, competitiveness and mood swings – classic childhood fallings-out – means that as they get older, and the stakes increase, they can debate with each other, and argue out a way forward, without damaging their friendship. Even in their bleakest moment, when in *The Deathly Hallows* Ron temporarily abandons Harry and Hermione, ostensibly out of frustration that they do not have a viable plan for finding and destroying the Horcruxes, Harry can see his point of view: 'He could not hide it from himself. Ron had been right.'[63] Hermione, in particular, successfully stops Harry's 'hot head' from dominating his 'good heart'. This crucial asset provides an illuminating contrast, in later chapters, to Voldemort's harsh treatment of his sycophantic inner circle (rather like the brutal way in which disagreements are handled in Gilead, see p. 177).

Thanks to the intimacy of boarding school (they are all members of the same House, Gryffindor), the friends soon become familiar with each other's strengths and weaknesses, and this familiarity develops from frustration to respect as all three use complementary skills to get out of trouble and they become an effective team. In *The Chamber of Secrets* Ron and Harry are initially comically baffled by Hermione's urgent need to find a book:

> 'Harry – I think I've just understood something! I've got to go to the library!' ...
>   '*What* does she understand?' said Harry, distractedly....
>   'Loads more than I do,' said Ron, shaking his head.
>   'But why's she got to go to the library?'
>   'Because that's what Hermione does,' said Ron, shrugging. 'When in doubt, go to the library.'[64]

But later in the series they appreciate her talent for researching leads and solving puzzles, which ultimately enables Harry to claim the most powerful wand in the magical world. In *The Philosopher's Stone* it is Ron's chess-playing ability that gets them through to the chamber in which the stone is hidden, and it is Harry's determination that brings that particular quest to its successful conclusion, as Hermione trusts it will:

'Harry – you're a great wizard, you know.'
   'I'm not as good as you,' said Harry, very embarrassed…
   'Me!' said Hermione. 'Books! And cleverness! There are more important things – friendship and bravery and – oh Harry – be *careful!*'[65]

Both Ron and Hermione use their best friends' intuition to give help to Harry when he himself is unable to ask for it. In a poignant scene, when Harry sees his parents' grave for the first time at Godric's Hollow and has nothing to lay at it, Hermione raises her wand and creates a wreath for him. On his return to them in *The Deathly Hallows*, Ron sees that Harry is struggling and he steps up and takes charge:

Perhaps because he was determined to make up for having walked out on them; perhaps because Harry's descent into listlessness galvanised his dormant leadership qualities, Ron was the one now encouraging and exhorting the other two into action.[66]

Like Frodo in *The Lord of the Rings*, Harry is constantly torn between appreciation of his friends' help and companionship and responsibility for their safety. Their first test comes in

The Philosopher's Stone when Harry tells them he is going through the trapdoor that night whatever anyone says, and Ron and Hermione insist they are coming too, even if they don't agree and it will mean a squeeze for all three to fit under the invisibility cloak. At the end of *The Half-Blood Prince*, the conversation is reprised when Ron tells Harry that he and Hermione are coming with him to find the Horcruxes (the hidden pieces of Voldemort's soul which must be destroyed):

> 'No – ' said Harry quickly; he had not counted on this, he had meant them to understand that he was undertaking this most dangerous journey alone.
>   'You said to us once before,' said Hermione quietly, 'that there was time to turn back if we wanted to. We've had time, haven't we?'
>   'We're with you whatever happens,' said Ron.[67]

Ironically, it is precisely this concern for friends that Voldemort, the Dark Lord, aims to exploit: 'Give me Harry Potter, and none shall be harmed.' This is how he persuades Harry to meet him alone in the Forbidden Forest.[68] But Voldemort – as Dumbledore, the wise headmaster of Hogwarts, points out – is incapable of love, and so does not understand its power in his opponent.

Though Harry does, ultimately, face Voldemort alone, while Ron and Hermione focus on destroying the last remaining Horcrux, he thinks of his friends as, prepared to die, he sets out to meet his nemesis:

> Ron and Hermione seemed a long way away, in a far-off country.... There would be no goodbyes, and no explanations, he was determined of that. This was a journey they could not take together...'[69]

However, his success is not only down to his own willingness to be sacrificed. It is also in no small measure thanks to their seven-year journey together, to Ron's destruction of Slytherin's locket and Hermione's of the Hufflepuff Cup, that Harry now has the wand, the wizardry and the wherewithal to destroy Voldemort. When he finally succeeds, it is of course his two incredible friends who reach him first, and it is they who embrace him and their shouts which celebrate his life-saving achievement.

Students & Apprentices

F RIENDSHIPS IN YOUNG ADULT LIFE are often tested by serious mistakes – reckless decisions stemming from inexperience and the exploration of identity. Prince Hamlet is still a student when faced with his uncle's treachery and both he and fellow scholar Horatio try to bring their learning to bear on a situation which requires political acumen rather than scholarship. Pip muddles through his apprenticeship in London, making false assumptions, neglecting his childhood friends, spending recklessly and almost ruining the forgiving friend who will ultimately pull him through. Charles looks on as his beautiful student friend Sebastian descends into alcoholism, paralysed by inexperience in the face of his friend's powerful family. Miss Brodie's 'set' believe themselves to be above conventional education. And the overconfidence of youthful friends perhaps reaches its zenith in *The Secret History*, when Richard Papen is so desperate to reinvent himself and be accepted by a sophisticated group of Classics students that he can cold-heartedly contemplate the murder of one of their number.

Prince and Philosopher

HAMLET & HORATIO

Hamlet by William Shakespeare

Hamlet, Prince of Denmark, learns from his dead
father's ghost that he has been murdered by Hamlet's
uncle, Claudius, who has now married Hamlet's mother
Gertrude and taken the throne. Hamlet must decide
whether and how to fulfil the ghost's command that he
avenge his father's death. Thinking he has caught Claudius
spying on him, he accidentally kills Polonius, father of
Ophelia and Laertes. This, coupled with Hamlet's sudden
coldness towards her, drives Ophelia to suicide. Claudius
manipulates grief-stricken Laertes into challenging Hamlet
to a duel to avenge the deaths of his father and sister by
fighting with a poisoned sword, but in the end the sword
is used on all three of them, with fatal consequences.
Hamlet's friend Horatio is left to recount the events to the
incoming Norwegian army.

Nobody knows exactly when WILLIAM SHAKESPEARE (1564–1616) wrote *Hamlet*, nor which of several different surviving versions of the play he would have regarded as definitive (the Bodleian Library holds an edition of the third quarto printed in 1611, as well as the version printed in the First Folio in 1623). The story comes from a Danish folk tale and the play has many similarities to Thomas Kyd's *The Spanish Tragedy*, performed around 1589. Some scholars think that Hamlet is named after Shakespeare's son, Hamnet, who died at the age of eleven. Shakespeare's *Hamlet* puts into play some of the theological concerns of the time, not least conflicting interpretations of the afterlife. Catholicism was at the time a banned religion in England; Elizabeth I was a Protestant queen and head of the Church of England. So, as scholars have pointed out, in the opening act the ghost is describing the Catholic landscape of purgatory to a student from a Protestant university who has been taught that such a place does not exist.

HAMLET is a student at Wittenberg, but his mother persuades him not to return there after his father's funeral. He is Prince of Denmark, but instead of inheriting the crown when his father dies he must instead swear allegiance to his uncle, who has married his mother. Hamlet is first stricken by grief for his father, then by guilt that he cannot avenge his death. He famously contemplates suicide. Although he is an accomplished swordsman, and fit from being in 'continual practice', he observes and tests his enemies before acting. He is well-read, and able to direct the travelling players who visit the court. Before the start of the play he has been wooing Ophelia, but the events surrounding his father's death cause him to reject her.

HORATIO is also at university in Wittenberg, the spiritual home of Martin Luther and the cradle of the Reformation. According to Hamlet he is a diligent scholar, and his measured, thoughtful approach to the extraordinary events he witnesses during the course of the play commands respect. Horatio often speaks in heightened poetic language, inspired by natural imagery, which lends gravitas to his character and draws in listeners. He successfully persuades Gertrude to grant an audience to the grieving Ophelia, and even Claudius calls him 'good Horatio'.

HAMLET ON HORATIO

Give me that man
That is not passion's slave, and I will wear him
In my heart's core, ay, in my heart of heart,
As I do thee.

HORATIO'S ROLE in this hugely complex and endlessly reinterpreted tragedy is a surprisingly passive one. A scholar from Wittenberg, he is most often in a scene to help interpret events, and not to fight alongside, rescue or defend his student friend Hamlet.

When Marcellus, a soldier on night watch, first tells Horatio about the ghost of Hamlet's father stalking the battlements, he refuses to believe it. Protestantism has taught him there is no such thing as purgatory, therefore ghosts – the manifestation of souls stuck between heaven and hell – cannot exist. But when Horatio witnesses it with his own eyes, he is the first to interpret a possible meaning for the ghost's appearance: 'this bodes some strange eruption to our state'.[1] Horatio has been brought to the scene because of his learning ('thou art a scholar – speak to it, Horatio'). He summarizes the dead king's career – the soldier who fought the Poles and killed the King of Norway – but his questions, about the fate of Denmark, about hidden loot, are not the right ones and elicit no answers. Once the ghost has disappeared, to comfort his friends and subdue their terror at witnessing this 'warlike' apparition, he resorts to describing what they can all see and recognize in gentle, poetic language:

> But look, the morn in russet mantle clad
> Walks o'er the dew of yon high eastern hill.
> Break we our watch up, and by my advice
> Let us impart what we have seen tonight
> Unto young Hamlet; for upon my life,
> This spirit, dumb to us, will speak to him.[2]

Because they are student friends, Horatio knows he must tell 'young Hamlet', not the queen, and not the king, about the haunting of the battlements. This decision sets in chain the tragic events of the drama.

Hamlet's affection and respect for Horatio are apparent from their first encounter in the play ('we'll teach you to drink deep ere you depart'[3]), so it is no surprise that he takes Horatio's account of the ghost seriously and decides to see for himself, in the company of his friend, later that night. Horatio warns him against following the ghost alone – he refers to it as a 'spirit' and is suspicious of its motivation: 'What if it tempt you toward the flood, my lord, / Or to the dreadful summit of the cliff...?'[4] But Horatio, perhaps a prototype of a 'bystander friend', is ultimately powerless to stop him, and so doesn't hear the full story of the king's murder until later in the play. Instead, he must trust his friend Hamlet when he instructs him to swear he will tell no one else of what he has seen. Horatio is uneasy

without a rational explanation, but Hamlet already understands
that their studies have not equipped them for this situation:

> HORATIO O day and night, but this is wondrous strange!
> HAMLET And therefore as a stranger give it welcome.
>   There are more things in heaven and earth, Horatio,
>   Than are dreamt of in our philosophy....[5]

Throughout the rest of the play, Horatio looks on (often
appearing after one of Hamlet's soliloquies, symbolizing his
trustworthiness), occasionally pointing out Hamlet's 'wild and
whirling words' or trying to calm his imagination: "Twere to
consider too curiously to consider so'.[6] Although he is the only
person in whom Hamlet confides, he doesn't offer advice, or
encourage Hamlet towards killing Claudius in revenge for his
father. After watching Claudius's extreme reaction to the play-
within-the-play (which re-enacts the murder) they have this
exchange, in which Horatio is careful not to draw conclusions:

> HAMLET O good Horatio, I'll take the Ghost's word for
>   a thousand pound. Didst perceive?
> HORATIO Very well, my lord.
> HAMLET Upon the talk of the pois'ning?
> HORATIO I did very well note him.[7]

It is Horatio to whom Hamlet sends his letter, after being
banished to England, warning of 'words to speak in thine ear
will make thee dumb',[8] and when Horatio hears these words
– describing how Hamlet found an instruction from Claudius,
ordering companions Rosencrantz and Guildenstern to murder
him, he exclaims, 'Why, what a king is this!' Even so, when

Hamlet asks 'is't not perfect conscience / To quit him with this arm?'[9] Horatio remains 'dumb', because he knows only Hamlet can answer that question.

Hamlet, by contrast, is only able to act definitively when he stops thinking so deeply about the consequences of revenge, or the nature of death, or the fragility of love. In the final scene, Horatio tries to stop him from fighting Laertes in the revenge duel set up by Claudius – 'If your mind dislike anything, obey it. I will forestall their repair hither, and say you are not fit' – an attempt to undermine the established, irrational convention of retribution. But Hamlet has by now reconciled himself to being unable to tell what the future will hold or what will happen after death, and he tells Horatio:

> If it be now, 'tis not to come. If it be not to come, it will be now. If it be not now, yet it will come. The readiness is all. Since no man has aught of what he leaves, what is't to leave betimes?[10]

Horatio's last act of friendship is to stay alive. He wants to take poison himself and die with his friend like an 'antique Roman', but Hamlet stops him. Instead of following the revenge tragedy trajectory and demanding his death be avenged, he begs Horatio to use his intellectual powers to faithfully recount what has happened:

> If thou didst ever hold me in thy heart,
> Absent thee from felicity a while
> And in this harsh world draw thy breath in pain
> To tell my story.[11]

Hamlet appeals to Horatio's 'heart', a word he has invoked previously to describe their friendship ('my heart's core'). Horatio responds by summoning up an image of beauty and comfort in the face of death, just as he has comforted the soldiers on the battlements with a description of the dawn at the start of the play:

> Good night, sweet prince,
> And flights of angels sing thee to thy rest.[12]

Horatio will survive to bear witness to his friend's story, 'lest more mischance / On plots and errors happen':

> So shall you hear
> Of carnal, bloody, and unnatural acts,
> Of accidental judgements, casual slaughters,
> Of deaths put on by cunning and forced cause;
> And, in this upshot, purposes mistook
> Fall'n on th'inventors' heads. All this can I
> Truly deliver.[13]

We know from his philosophical and rational stance throughout the play, and his affection for Hamlet, that Horatio's account – surrounded by dead bodies and the newly arrived soldiers from Norway – is the best hope of bringing an end to the cycle of violence and revenge.

HORATIO ON HAMLET
Now cracks a noble heart.

Career Advice

PIP *&* HERBERT

Great Expectations by Charles Dickens

A coming-of-age novel following the fortunes of Pip, from his childhood meeting with an escaped convict on the misty Kent marshes to his adoration of the unattainable Estella and his escapades in the City of London.

CHARLES DICKENS (1812–1870) began writing *Great Expectations* in the autumn of 1860, at the age of forty-eight. It was published in instalments in his magazine *All the Year Round* from December 1860 to August 1861 and then as a novel in three volumes. The London setting draws on Dickens's experience as a young reporter before his literary career took off; the Kent marshes were familiar to him from a childhood spent around Chatham. In the first draft ending, Estella marries a doctor after the death of her abusive first husband. But, on the advice of his friends, Dickens changed this to a hint that Pip and Estella might end up together at last.

Orphaned as a baby, PIP (PHILIP PIRRIP) has been brought up by his sister and her husband, Joe, a blacksmith, who protects Pip from his sister's violent temper. When Pip is invited to Miss Havisham's house and meets the beautiful Estella, however, he becomes ashamed of his humble origins and aspires to wealth and a high position in society instead of an apprenticeship at the forge. Young Pip generally does what he is told: he steals food when commanded to do so by the convict Magwitch, he visits Miss Havisham on his Uncle Pumblechook's recommendation, he falls in love with Estella on Miss Havisham's encouragement. Older Pip only learns how to take control of his life fully when he accepts his position in society and no longer expects an inheritance.

Young HERBERT POCKET is afflicted by pimples, paleness and red eyelids. But he grows up blessed with a countenance that is 'extremely amiable and cheerful' and a figure that would 'always be light and young'.[14] He is good at rowing and bad at fighting. The Pocket family is based in Hammersmith, but Herbert is keen to be independent of his lineage-obsessed mother and distracted father, not to mention all the little Pockets who are 'tumbling up' despite their mother's absent-minded neglect. Herbert has his own nickname for Pip – Handel – to signify harmony. He is secretly betrothed to Clara Barley, knowing that his parents will not approve of the match. By the end of the book he is a partner at the shipping merchants Clarriker's.

PIP ON HERBERT

Herbert Pocket had a frank and easy way with him that was very taking. I had never seen anyone then, and I have never seen anyone since, who more strongly expressed to me, in every look and tone, a natural incapacity to do anything secret and mean.

HERBERT ON PIP

A good fellow, with impetuosity and hesitation, boldness and diffidence, action and dreaming, curiously mixed in him.

HOST, MENTOR, CONFIDANT, nurse: who wouldn't want a friend like Herbert Pocket? The newly wealthy young hero Pip, arriving in London to learn how to be a gentleman, couldn't have wished for a better room-mate in Barnard's Inn.

Of a similar age, and in similar circumstances – both are young bachelors looking to embark on a career – the two men take an instant liking to each other. This is made all the more charming by their realization that they have met several years earlier, in the overgrown garden belonging to rich Miss Havisham, where, on first sight, Herbert (the 'pale young gentleman') challenged Pip (the 'prowling boy') to a fight.[15] The fight itself is conducted with comical decorum: Herbert stakes out the ground and provides water and a sponge soaked in vinegar for them both to use. After Pip's punches have floored Herbert several times, they shake hands and bid each other 'Good afternoon'. It's an odd scene in the spooky setting of Miss Havisham's derelict estate, and it's a clever way of setting up the friendship. Any potential rivalry – Hebert has been invited to Miss Havisham's, just as Pip has, to provide her with amusement on the expectation of a reward – is disposed of swiftly in a physical contest and it feels right that Pip, deemed the underdog at the time because he is from the smithy and Herbert is wearing a suit, should win it. He also earns a kiss from the aloof Estella, who has been secretly watching them.

But although Pip has superior strength and, by the time of their first meeting in London, superior funds from a mysterious benefactor, he needs Herbert's knowledge of how to behave in society and navigate the City of London in order to hide his humble origins and progress in his career. 'He carried off his rather old clothes much better than I carried off my new suit',[16] Pip observes, and learns from Herbert not to put his knife in his mouth or stuff his napkin into his tumbler. He has a hunch that Herbert 'would never be very successful or rich'[17] and so feels quite unthreatened by his superior manners. He finds it much easier to aspire to a friendship with someone he perceives as socially superior to him than to maintain his friendship with kind Joe Gargery from the forge, a part of his life he can't wait to leave behind.

In a novel that is peppered with misguided, treacherous or neglected friendships, Pip and Herbert's is one of honesty and constancy. They hit the town together, row on the Thames together, confide in each other about their love for Estella (Pip) and Clara (Herbert) respectively, move lodgings, fall into debt and solve the mystery of Miss Havisham's swindling fiancé together. Herbert embodies the constant helpfulness, resourcefulness and companionship that everyone wants in a friend. He nurses Pip's burns after Miss Havisham sets herself and her desolate house on fire; he follows Pip on his reckless visit to the limekilns with an instinct that he is in danger and rescues him from a near-fatal attack by the murderous Orlick; he even accompanies him to Mr Wopsle's tedious amateur dramatics.

As their friendship deepens, their fortunes become inextricably connected. Pip leads Herbert astray somewhat with his now extravagant lifestyle, encouraging him to run up debts and keep late hours. But as soon as Pip learns he will receive £500 a year on reaching the age of twenty-one, his immediate thought is how he can use his money to help Herbert, who has been thwarted in his ambitions in the City by a lack of connection in the insurance world. Pip secretly pays for a position and shares in the enjoyment of his friend's success:

> Day by day as his hopes grew stronger and his face brighter, he must have thought me a more and more affectionate friend, for I had the greatest difficulty in restraining my tears of triumph when I saw him so happy. At length, the thing being done, and he having that day entered Clarriker's House, and he having talked to me for a whole evening in a flush of pleasure and success, I did really cry in good earnest when I went to bed, to think that my expectations had done some good to somebody.[18]

Pip most appreciates the nature of their friendship when the true identity of his benefactor is revealed to him: not the socially superior Miss Havisham after all, but the convict Magwitch, whom Pip helped as a young boy so many years ago. He longs for Herbert to return from business in Cairo to share with him this life-changing and socially devastating news and seek his advice. When they are finally alone together, Pip 'had never felt before so blessedly what it is to have a friend'.[19]

Unlike Pip, Herbert is neither put off by humble origins nor paralysed by his expectations: as soon as a door is opened for him, he makes the most of the opportunity, and ultimately helps his friend to do so, too, by finding him work when his fortune is lost. Dickens uses Herbert's loyalty to encourage us to sympathize with Pip even when he makes selfish decisions and neglects, out of snobbery, the friendship of his kind brother-in-law Joe, who remains constant throughout – 'ever the best of friends' – however uncomfortable Pip makes him feel. It is through Herbert's model behaviour that Pip finally comes to some self-knowledge and we like him better for it:

> We owed so much to Herbert's ever cheerful industry and readiness, that I often wondered how I had conceived that old idea of his inaptitude, until I was one day enlightened by the reflection, that perhaps the inaptitude had never been in him at all, but had been in me.[20]

A Bystander's Elegy

CHARLES & SEBASTIAN

Brideshead Revisited by Evelyn Waugh

Charles Ryder meets Lord Sebastian Flyte at Oxford and they form a close bond. But as Charles gradually becomes close to the Marchmains, Sebastian's complex and extraordinary family, Sebastian himself retreats from them and descends into alcoholism. Society is changing fast, and the world moves swiftly towards war, but the Marchmain family's Catholic faith continues to tie them to each other and their ancestral home of Brideshead Castle.

EVELYN WAUGH (1903–1966) wrote *Brideshead Revisited* in 1944, on leave from the army due to a broken leg. It was published in May 1945, during the final year of the Second World War. The reminiscences described in Waugh's autobiography, *A Little Learning*, show how he drew on his memories of Oxford when writing the novel (he had been an undergraduate at Hertford College), in particular his close relationships with Richard Pares and Alastair Graham. Indeed, the name Alastair features instead of Sebastian in some parts of the original manuscript.[21] Waugh converted to Catholicism in 1930, six years after leaving Oxford without taking a degree.

SEBASTIAN FLYTE has an androgynous and arresting beauty. His charm is dazzling and wins him affection wherever he goes. He has dark hair, dresses in fine clothes ('dove-grey flannel, white *crêpe de Chine*') and adores beautiful things.[22] In his first year at Oxford, Sebastian is inseparable from his teddy bear Aloysius, and belongs, according to Charles's cousin Jasper, to the '*very worst set in the University*'.[23] He is the second youngest of the four Marchmain children.

CHARLES RYDER is an only child whose mother died during the First World War, when he was very young. He has led a sheltered and lonely existence at his father's house and then boarding school and has very little experience of female company (his father is a misanthropist whose behaviour drove his kindly aunt from the family home). Interested in painting, he is not yet sure of his taste in art and artefacts, but he shares Sebastian's love of beauty. Like Sebastian he is nineteen years old when their friendship begins, but relates the story looking back from a perspective of twenty years.

Et in Arcadia Ego.

IT ONLY TAKES UP the first third of the book, but it is the beautifully warm, empathetic and exquisitely sad portrayal of Charles and Sebastian's intense friendship which is the enduring image of *Brideshead Revisited*. Why is it that this ultimately doomed relationship between two young men should resonate so strongly? First, we are being shown the friendship from a nostalgic point of view: a man, now 'homeless, childless, middle-aged' and 'loveless',[24] looking back on his student days, twenty years ago. What's more, he is now a member of the British Army during the worst conflict the country has ever experienced, and he is reminiscing about peacetime – interwar Britain in fact – when, in his circle at least, there was no rationing, no bomb damage, no indication of the horrors to come. Second, he is describing to us a friendship formed at the age of nineteen, at university, a brief, temporary period of life before the responsibilities of work and family dominate. And, lastly, he is in mourning for a friendship he has now lost forever. All of these elements suffuse the first part of the book with an exquisite, elegiac quality against the beautiful backdrops of Oxford in the 1920s and the fictional Brideshead Castle.

'I was in search of love in those days,' writes Charles, as he sets out to have lunch for the first time in Sebastian's rooms at Christ Church, 'and I went full of curiosity and the faint, unrecognized apprehension that here, at last, I should find that low door in the wall ... which opened on an enclosed and enchanted garden, which was somewhere ... in the heart of that grey city.'[25] Perhaps, at the age of nineteen, in an all-male Oxford college, the capacity to form close friendships was like falling in love – a 'forerunner' as Charles later says, to marriage. Despite an inauspicious first encounter (so often the way with an intense new friendship), when, late one evening, Sebastian leans through Charles's ground-floor window and throws up, Sebastian and Charles become inseparable – getting drunk together, picnicking together, sunbathing in the nude, sharing a bathroom at Brideshead. Is it a sexual relationship? Waugh does not say that it is – at that time, homosexuality was criminalized – and certainly Cara, Lord Marchmain's 'mistress', regards it as an adolescent phase: 'I know of these romantic friendships of the English... I think they are very good if they do not go on too long... It is better to have that kind of love for another boy than for a girl.'[26] But Charles also admits, later in life, that one of his reasons for marrying a woman he doesn't like is because he misses Sebastian.

During this time, it seems always to be summer. When we first meet Sebastian, he has borrowed a two-seater Morris Cowley, stocked it with strawberries and a bottle of Château Peyraguey and is rescuing Charles from a college overrun with preparations for a May ball. Charles, the archetypal 'bystander' friend, cannot help but be intoxicated and remains so throughout the rest of his first summer term at Oxford, sampling champagne, lobster Newburg and plovers' eggs with Sebastian and whiling away the afternoons at the Botanic Garden.

Charles's unhappy childhood is mirrored by Sebastian's reluctance to let his go (hence the teddy bear and the visits to Nanny Hawkins), and Charles feels compensated for his by the extravagance he learns from his friend – silk shirts, cigars and liqueurs take the place of childhood toys. Their pursuit of pleasure continues in the summer vacation at Brideshead, where Charles helps Sebastian recuperate from an injured foot and they have the run of the house and grounds with no family present and no obligations. Their days are spent harvesting figs, orchids and grapes from the abundant gardens; their evenings in sampling the vintage wines from the capacious cellars, resulting in much endearing hilarity:

'It is a little, shy wine like a gazelle.'
    'Like a leprechaun.'
    'Dappled, in a tapestry meadow.'
    'Like a flute by still water.'

Sated with wine, they sit by the fountain under the stars, and Charles savours such moments so intensely that when Sebastian asks him if they ought really to get drunk every night his reply is: 'Yes, I think so.' Sebastian, though, is already anticipating the moment when this heavenly existence will come to an end: 'If it could only be like this always – always summer, always alone, the fruit always ripe…'[27]

This idyllic phase of their friendship, when Charles believes himself to be 'very near heaven', lasts only for four terms and a summer; on return to Oxford after the Christmas of their second year, Sebastian is already on borrowed time for a drink-driving conviction and showing signs of depression and a desire to drink alone. Cara has predicted this during their visit to Venice and warns Charles: 'I see it in the *way* Sebastian drinks. It is not your way.'[28] But it takes Charles a long time to realize how serious his friend's alcoholism is.

The Marchmain family, however, having seen Lord Marchmain also struggle with drink, are under no such illusion. Lady Marchmain tries to recruit Charles to her controlling way of dealing with her son – 'Sebastian is fonder of you than any of us, you know. You've got to help him.' – and for a while he treads a delicate path between loyalty to Sebastian and responsibility to the family, in the end helping neither: 'I had seen him grow wary at the thought of his family or his religion, now I found I, too, was suspect,' Charles explains. 'As my intimacy with his family grew, I became part of the world which he sought to escape.'[29]

Sebastian's drinking is inextricably bound up with his position in his family, his mother and his religion. Charles tries to explain it to Lady Marchmain – 'he's ashamed of being unhappy' – and to convince her that she (being part of the problem) should leave Sebastian alone. Reluctant to take action, and so alienate his friend further, he begins to mourn him, even while they are still together: 'He was sick at heart somewhere, I did not know how, and I grieved for him, unable to help.'[30]

Charles promises Lady Marchmain, in good faith, that Sebastian is not binge-drinking in their second year at Oxford and is undermined when Sebastian gets plastered that very night and is found by the junior dean. The consequence of this is that they have one last defiant night of inebriation in Oxford before leaving without taking their degrees: Charles in a positive move to attend art school, Sebastian to a tour of the Eastern Mediterranean with a scholarly minder, from whom inevitably he escapes in order to drink again.

Charles's final, 'callously wicked' act, in the eyes of Lady Marchmain, is to give Sebastian money the following Christmas, knowing he will ride over to the nearest pub and spend the afternoon 'soaking' in the bar.[31] On the one hand, this is irresponsible collusion with an addict. On the other, it is done out of love and a desire to protect his friend from his manipulative mother and what Charles sees then (though he will later take a different view) as the destructive influence of his religion. He doesn't make excuses for his own mistakes as he recounts these sad episodes, but he does convey poignantly the excruciating pain of observing his friend's descent into alcoholism and his own inability, at the naive age of twenty, to stop it:

> A blow, expected, repeated, falling on a bruise, with no smart or shock of surprise, only a dull and sickening pain and the doubt whether another like it could be borne – that was how it felt, sitting opposite Sebastian at dinner that night, seeing his clouded eye and groping movements, hearing his thickened voice...[32]

Charles asks Sebastian outright whether there is any use him being there, and the answer comes back, 'No help.' But, as Charles leaves Brideshead Castle for what he thinks will be the last time, he already knows that he will long for this friendship all his life:

> I felt that I was leaving part of myself behind, and that wherever I went afterwards I should feel the lack of it, and search for it hopelessly, as ghosts are said to do, frequenting the spots where they buried material treasures without which they cannot pay their way to the nether world.[33]

Charles makes one last attempt to rescue his friend when he learns that Lady Marchmain is dying. Sebastian, emaciated by drink, is by then living in Fez with an invalid ex-mercenary. Charles tries to persuade him to come home but Sebastian is ill himself, being treated by monks in an infirmary, while also smuggling in bottles of brandy. Charles concludes, sadly, 'There was nothing more I could do for Sebastian', and instead of trying to cure him resigns himself instead to practical help, making sure Sebastian's allowance from the family is managed properly at the local bank.

Nevertheless, after a failed marriage and ten years as an artist, Charles knows that he has 'never ... come alive as I had been during the time of my friendship with Sebastian'.[34] He seeks it in his affair with Sebastian's sister, Julia, but in the end she too is claimed by her religion. On hearing the final account of Sebastian – a dishevelled and drunken hanger-on at a monastery in Tunisia, slowly dying of his addiction – Charles prefers to remember 'the youth with the teddy-bear under the flowering chestnuts', whose student innocence he was unable to preserve.[35]

Crème de la Crème

SANDY, JENNY, EUNICE, MARY, MONICA, ROSE & MISS BRODIE

The Prime of Miss Jean Brodie by Muriel Spark

Miss Jean Brodie cultivates a hand-picked group of girls from her class at an all-girls school in Edinburgh in the 1930s. At first they love being in her 'set', invited to tea at her house and taken on exclusive expeditions to the galleries and theatre. But as they reach puberty, her behaviour becomes disturbingly manipulative.

MURIEL SPARK (1918–2006) had already published five novels before *The Prime of Miss Jean Brodie* appeared, first printed in the *New Yorker* in 1961. The eponymous teacher is partly inspired by Miss Christina Kay, who taught Spark at James Gillespie's High School for Girls in Edinburgh and who Spark later described as 'that character in search of an author'.[36] The teacher was memorably portrayed by Maggie Smith in the film adaptation of the book, released in 1969.

MISS JEAN BRODIE, a teacher in the junior department of the Marcia Blaine School for Girls, is in her early forties. She has brown hair coiled at the nape of her neck, brown eyes and a fleeting beauty. She is slim, straight-backed and tanned from European holidays.

She wears brown skirts, suffers from an 'excessive lack of guilt' and declares herself to be in her 'prime'.[37]

SANDY STRANGER is admired for her beautiful pronunciation and ability to recite. She has small, pig-like eyes (Teddy Lloyd, the art teacher, thinks she is ugly) and a habit of peering at people. She develops an interest in psychology and religion and eventually becomes a nun. When she is younger, she daydreams about the hero of *Kidnapped*.

JENNY GRAY is the prettiest of the set and has beautiful curls. She has a lovely singing voice and is admired for her elocution. When younger, Jenny and Sandy delight in writing secret fictional accounts of Miss Brodie's lovers.

MARY MACGREGOR is dull and as featureless as a snowman – 'a silent lump, a nobody whom everybody could blame'.[38] She thinks that Latin and shorthand are the same thing. She is destined to die young, at the age of twenty-three.

EUNICE GARDINER is small and neat and can do the splits. She excels at gymnastics and swimming. In her religious phase she turns temporarily nasty; she is the first of the set to have a boyfriend.

MONICA DOUGLAS is brilliant at mental arithmetic and becomes a prefect. She is prone to slapping when she gets angry, has a red nose, long dark plaits and 'peg-like' legs. She witnesses Miss Brodie kissing Mr Lloyd in the art room.

ROSE STANLEY is blonde, pale-skinned and 'famous for sex-appeal'.[39] She likes the cinema and is mature for her age. On leaving school, she sheds Miss Brodie's influence 'as a dog shakes pond-water from its coat'.[40]

Muriel Spark's darkly comic virtuoso portrait of a charismatic teacher and the girls in her charge is a brilliant dissection of what it is like to be in a clique, 'the Brodie set' in fact, especially one that has been chosen for you at school, and to which you belong without really knowing how you got there.

Miss Brodie instils a sense of superiority in the girls, whom she famously describes as the 'crème de la crème'. They enjoy their reputation for being the chosen ones in the school, and like the fact that 'everyone thought the Brodie set had more fun than anyone else'.[41] Lessons with Miss Brodie in junior school certainly are more fun than doing grammar and arithmetic: she tells them captivating stories of her former lovers, accounts of her holidays in Italy and Egypt and of her own eclectic role models: Anna Pavlova, Sibyl Thorndike, Helen of Troy and, disturbingly, Mussolini.

Sandy and her best friend Jenny are initially inspired by their teacher's romantic reminiscences and write their own steamy versions of her love affairs. The example she sets, however, and which she expects her girls to follow, is flawed and ultimately dangerous. Sandy, in particular, has doubts early on, as she feels that Miss Brodie's influence extends beyond her favoured subjects of the arts and music to control relationships within the set itself; she even likens the set to the fascisti, whom Miss Brodie misguidedly admires. On a walk into Edinburgh, Sandy has an urge to be nice to Mary Macgregor – the scapegoat of the set – because it would make her feel better about herself. But Miss Brodie's domineering tones interrupt her and cause her to be frightened of her instinct in case it separates her from the set: 'she would ... be lonely, and blameable in a more dreadful way than Mary who, although officially the faulty one, was at least inside Miss Brodie's category of heroines in the making.' So, she defaults to learned behaviour and instead says something nasty to Mary, who cries. Similarly, when Miss Brodie denounces the Guides, Sandy is rebelliously tempted to try to join the Brownies. But then 'the group-fright seized her again, and it was necessary to put the idea aside, because she loved Miss Brodie.'[42]

Miss Brodie's influence is a complex mix of generosity, hospitality, seductive confidences, overconfident opinions and dangerous politics. When the girls leave junior school Miss Brodie carefully retains their loyalty: 'she described some of her new little girls and made the old ones laugh, which bound her set together more than ever and made them feel chosen.'[43] They continue to visit Miss Brodie at her home, and later at the home of her lover, the music teacher, once they have left junior school, and she binds them together further by telling them about her fellow conventional teachers' 'plots' against her, while simultaneously criticizing individual girls behind their backs. As they reach their teenage years it is the idea of the set that keeps them together, rather than any proactive desire on their part, and by the age of sixteen they have 'very little in common with each other outside their continuing friendship with Jean Brodie', and a group loyalty which protects her from the increasing scrutiny of the headmistress.[44] The structure of the book, which early on in the narrative gives us vignettes of the girls' very different adult lives but then flits back in time to scenes at the school, underscores the feeling that their teacher's influence, and therefore that of the six friends, prevails in their memories even when their schooldays are long gone. This disorientating technique also reflects how hard it is, when young, to realise how wrong a friend who is older, charismatic and in authority can be.

Sandy, increasingly drawn to science rather than stories, sees that their reputation as the Brodie set now means that they can never escape it, since it is so firmly rooted in everyone's mind. Teddy Lloyd, the art teacher and Miss Brodie's former lover, wants to paint a group portrait of the girls, which Sandy fears will somehow freeze them in time as an inseparable group, thwarting their emerging sense of individualism. The headmistress, Miss Mackay, also finds the clique impossible to penetrate: 'By the time their friendship with Miss Brodie was of seven-years standing, it had worked itself into their bones, so that they could not break away without, as it were, splitting their bones to do so.'[45]

Perhaps this is partly what motivates Sandy, at the age of eighteen, to begin an affair with Teddy Lloyd, Miss Brodie's former lover, even though she knows that Miss Brodie is angling for Rose to become his lover so that she can vicariously enjoy stories of the romance, and Sandy herself has become a trusted friend of Teddy Lloyd's wife and children. Perhaps it is partly that she sees Teddy Lloyd is still in love with Miss Brodie, and she resents it, especially when every portrait he paints, even of Rose in the nude, ends up as a likeness of Miss Brodie. But it is also Miss Brodie's modelling of self-confidence, belief in making the most of her 'prime' and an absence of guilt which give Sandy the wherewithal to take such a bold step.

Miss Brodie's final and fatal accomplishment is, therefore, to create a pupil with similar depths of guilt-free self-confidence to her own – enough, in fact, for this young woman to finally betray the friend and formative influence of her first twenty years. It is Sandy who, in the end, gives Miss Mackay a good enough reason to dismiss Miss Brodie. Not, after all, for her love affairs, or her unorthodox teaching methods, but for her dangerous promotion of Fascism to the young girls in her care.

In adult life, the girls individually visit Sandy in her nunnery, as if she has now usurped the teacher in becoming the focal point of their set. Their conversation always comes back to some aspect of Miss Brodie, however, not knowing who betrayed her (tellingly, Sandy, still in thrall to the Brodie set, never admits what she did), speculating whether their teacher was a sinner or just 'marvellous fun', inspirational or manipulative, 'full of fight' or, in the end, 'past her prime'. Eunice lays flowers at her grave. Sandy wonders 'to what extent it was Miss Brodie who had developed complications throughout the years, and to what extent it was her own conception of Miss Brodie that had changed'.[46] It takes twenty-five years before Sandy, now the author of a successful book on psychology, can see beyond the 'tiresome woman' she so confidently betrayed in early adulthood, and recognize that, however uncomfortable it may be to admit it, in order for her to intervene as she did, Miss Brodie's 'defective sense of self-criticism had not been without its beneficent and enlarging effects'.[47]

Campus Collusion

RICHARD, BUNNY, FRANCIS, CAMILLA, CHARLES & HENRY

The Secret History by Donna Tartt

A highbrow thriller about five students – all studying Classics at the fictional campus university Hampden College – and how they came to murder their friend Bunny Corcoran.

DONNA TARTT has described *The Secret History* as a 'whydunit', as opposed to a 'whodunit', since we are told who murdered Bunny in the opening pages.[48] She graduated from Bennington College in Vermont (where the fictional Hampden College is located), studying there at the same time as novelist Brett Easton Ellis (to whom *The Secret History* is dedicated). She began work on the novel while still a student, but it wasn't published until 1992, when she was twenty-eight. An instant success, it has sold over 5 million copies and been translated into multiple languages.

RICHARD PAPEN, the narrator of the story, is the 'bystander' character, and has been compared to Charles Ryder in *Brideshead Revisited*. Now aged twenty-eight, he grew up in California. Though he won't admit it to his new rich friends, his father owns a petrol station and his mother is a receptionist. Like Henry and Francis, he is an only child. Though he is tall and has prominent freckles, he is very good at being unnoticeable. He is determined to leave his past life in California behind and reinvent himself at college, using his talent for lying. He suffers from insomnia.

BUNNY (EDMUND) CORCORAN is large and loud: six foot three with a honking voice, sandy hair, tweed jacket and rosy cheeks. He is dyslexic and asthmatic. Although he has expensive tastes in clothes and restaurants, he cannot afford to pay the bills. He has attended exclusive private schools but never been given an allowance, since his parents, too, pretend to be rich when actually they are almost bankrupt. Bunny steals food and minor items; he teases his friends and doesn't stop when they are obviously in discomfort. He follows a regular routine and has a girlfriend outside of 'the group'.

FRANCIS ABERNATHY has a pale face and red hair. Richard thinks he is 'angular and elegant', but he also has a 'quick temper' and a 'sharp tongue'. He suffers from stress and hypochondria. From a wealthy family, Francis has grown up in Boston; his mother is young and has a new boyfriend; his aunt owns a house in the countryside not far from Hampden. Francis is gay and has slept with Charles.

CHARLES MACAULAY has dark blond hair and often wears white or pale clothes. He is naturally friendly, but he suffers from gloomy spells. He plays the piano, always cooks dinner for everyone on Sunday nights and drinks the most alcohol of all the friends. Charles becomes jealous of his twin sister, Camilla, and it is rumoured that they occasionally sleep together. Richard likes the twins best: 'Charles had ... a way of showing up in my room, or turning to me in a crowd with a tranquil assumption – heart warming to me – that he and I were particular friends.'[49]

CAMILLA MACAULAY has gold hair with little curls that frame her face (a Dionysian feature) and her cheeks are often flushed. She has 'iron-coloured' eyes and wears soft pale woollen jumpers and white scarves. She can be aloof and manipulative – on their first encounter she smiles at Richard 'as if I were a waiter or a clerk in a store'.[50] Nevertheless, Richard is very attracted to Camilla.

HENRY WINTER is over six foot tall and well built. He has dark hair, a square jaw and blue eyes (over which he wears round steel glasses). He wears suits and often carries an umbrella. Like Richard, he has an ability to melt into the shadows when necessary. He is also an insomniac and suffers from intense migraines. Of independent means, Henry studies for the pure pleasure of it, not to gain qualifications. His trust fund means that he will never need to work. He is the most well-read and deemed the most intelligent of the students in the Greek class. But he also fiercely protects his own privacy.

A SIDE FROM the not insignificant fact that the prologue contains a confession of murder, the first part of this novel is a familiar set-up. A young man, keen to escape from a modest background, arrives at university and must navigate a new set of acquaintances from different social strata. Richard's description of freshers' week – 'I made some friends, most of them freshmen … *Friends* is perhaps an inaccurate word to use. We … mainly were thrown together' – is rather dismissive (and reminiscent of Jasper's advice to Charles in *Brideshead Revisited*), and he quickly grows to despise the drink- and drug-fuelled Friday night campus parties. It only takes him a couple of weeks to become fascinated by a self-contained group of Classics students and to engineer an introduction to them

instead. It is entirely apt that his first encounter with them is
described in terms of art: 'it was as if the characters in a favorite
painting, absorbed in their own concerns, had looked up out of
the canvas and spoken to me.' All six friends are obsessed by
aesthetics and this in turn is bound up with their intensive study
of Greek under their charismatic and unconventional tutor,
Julian Morrow, who has more than a hint of Miss Jean Brodie
about him. Much of the book is a portrait of this close-knit
group and the dangerous power engendered by their communal
feeling of superiority over their peers.[51]

Before things go disastrously wrong, the friends enjoy an
idyllic student existence, lounging around at Francis's aunt's
house, reading, playing cards, going for walks and picnics,
rowing on the lake, drinking to excess and eschewing contemporary entertainment such as television, video games and student
bops (this is the decade before mobile phones and widespread
internet reach). Richard wants it to go on forever:

> The idea of living there, of not having to go back ever
> again to asphalt and shopping malls and modular furniture;
> of living there with Charles and Camilla and Henry and
> Francis and maybe even Bunny; of no one marrying or going
> home or getting a job ... the idea was so truly heavenly
> that I'm not sure I thought, even then, it could ever really
> happen, but I like to believe I did.[52]

But slowly, inexorably, the beautiful new world that has
so intoxicated Richard starts to unravel. First, he foolishly
decides to stay in Hampden over the winter holidays, and
the cold climate of Vermont almost kills him in his unheated

accommodation. It is Henry, returning early from a disastrous holiday with Bunny, who finds Richard shivering in his digs and takes him to hospital, where he is treated for pneumonia. Richard, the outsider, the newest recruit to the class, is now more indebted than ever to the friendship. What he doesn't know until almost halfway through the book is that his new friends have accidentally killed a local man while attempting to stage a bacchanal (an Ancient Greek rite, named after Bacchus or Dionysus, the god of wine, in which participants lose all inhibitions due to alcohol, dancing and drugs) in the woods around Francis's aunt's house. Bunny was not with them when this happened, but he has guessed the truth, and is more or less blackmailing them.

Richard has by now become so interwoven into the group – invited to their regular Sunday-night dinner at Charles and Camilla's, to weekends at Francis's aunt's house and to trips into town – and is so desperate to remain part of this exclusive circle that when they eventually let him in on the secret he finds it almost easy to assimilate their horrific disclosure:

> 'It doesn't matter.' I said this without thinking, but as soon as I had, I realized, with something of a jolt, that it was true; it really didn't matter that much, at least not in the preconceived way that one would expect.[53]

At this point, Richard is still so keen to keep hold of his new friends that he will accept almost anything. Later, he puts this down to a 'hideous pack instinct which would enable me to fall into step without question', like an inebriated follower of Bacchus himself.[54]

Still, it is a while before their solution to the situation – that they must kill Bunny to stop him from turning them in for murder – becomes inevitable. Initially it is a waiting game, during which Richard observes the speedy deterioration of Bunny's mental health. This manifests itself in personal, racist insults, an intensified version of the teasing and needling he'd always indulged in, coercion, and more drunkenness than usual. Some of this is directed at Richard, which he later uses as justification for the way he sides with the others against Bunny. As Richard himself admits, this behaviour is not enough to justify cold-blooded murder carried out by five rational, intelligent people, but, let in on their secret, we as readers are now invested in this group of friends, and as the compelling narrative progresses we cannot help but want them to get away with it, in danger of becoming part of the pack ourselves.

Although all the friends are in it together, it is Henry who comes up with the carefully researched ideas – first an elaborate scheme involving poison, then the simpler plan of making a fatal fall appear like an accident. Unlike Francis, Charles and Camilla, who all experience extreme guilt, stress, paranoia and anxiety, Henry remains calm and logical, able to regard the situation as a 'chess problem'. Richard, also, wonders at his own ability to remain normal, and later, after Bunny's death, Henry draws attention to their similar knack for detachment, what could in fact be viewed as a psychopathic characteristic, in this exchange:

'You don't feel a great deal of emotion for other people, do you?'
  I was taken aback. 'What are you talking about?' I said. 'Of
course I do.'
'Do you?' He raised an eyebrow. 'I don't think so. It doesn't
matter,' he said, after a long, tense pause. 'I don't, either.' [55]

Towards the end of the book, Richard's girlfriend Sophie
will give him a similar reason for splitting up with him:
'I was uncommunicative, she said. She never knew what I was
thinking. The way I looked at her sometimes, when I woke up
in the morning, frightened her.'[56] Have we, by engaging with
his narrative, befriended a psychopath?

Richard himself, despite his horror at being compared to
Henry, realizes that there is a limit, after all, to what friendship can endure, and that once you are part of the pack it is
impossible to leave it if you change your mind:

> At one time I had liked the idea, that the act, at least, had
> bound us together; we were not ordinary friends, but friends till
> death-do-us-part. … Now it made me sick, knowing there was
> no way out. I was stuck with them, with all of them, for good.[57]

At the end of the story Henry has taken his own life and,
though never arrested for their crime, the four remaining
friends are stuck in a kind of purgatory: Francis is suicidal
and trapped in a loveless heterosexual marriage; Charles is
suffering from severe alcoholism; Camilla cares full-time for
her ageing grandmother. Richard makes one last attempt to
form a relationship with Camilla, but she rejects him for the
memory of Henry. Richard himself is friendless and living back

in California, the very place he tried so hard to leave behind when he made his fateful application to Hampden College.

The 'friends' Richard made during freshers' week, only to speedily ditch them in favour of the Greek class, all, inevitably, fare rather better, having survived their own twentieth-century 'bacchanals' of drug and alcohol-fuelled student bops (without killing anyone) and gone on to fit right into the modern working world.

Heart to Heart

T HE FEMALE FRIENDSHIPS which coalesce around romantic plot lines are complex. On the one hand, to admit that you have fallen in love requires a deep trust in a friend; on the other, the navigation of how to develop or fulfil the romantic relationship brings to the fore many vulnerabilities and limitations imposed by society. With her friend Celia's help, Rosalind adopts a male disguise in order to behave as she pleases and cross-examine her lover; Emma tries – and fails – to control matchmaking in her society, partly because of a secret engagement formed to avoid social disapproval, which also thwarts a potential friendship. Maggie's fierce independence brings her in direct opposition to Victorian society, which punishes her for being attractive to the wrong man and jeopardizes her relationship with her beloved cousin Lucy. Even in the 1990s Bridget's friends are still complaining about the 'smug marrieds' who look down on them for not having partners, and Bridget has to explain patiently to her conservative mother that her lack of a boyfriend is 'a social trend'. Ironically, the heart-to-hearts these friends have about being in love tell us more about the position of women in society than they do about their particular objects of desire.

Inseparable

CELIA & ROSALIND

As You Like It by William Shakespeare

Duke Frederick (Celia's father) has exiled his brother, Duke Senior (Rosalind's father), to the Forest of Arden, though Rosalind remains at court. Following a boxing match at which Rosalind supports the winner, Orlando (a loyal follower of her father), Duke Frederick decides to exile her, too, and Celia goes with her. In the Forest they adopt disguises: Rosalind becomes a boy, Ganymede, and Celia becomes Aliena, his sister. Orlando has also fled to the Forest, following a row with his brother Oliver, and both parties encounter the exiled Duke and his men. Rosalind encourages Orlando to confess his love for her while she pretends to be a boy pretending to be Rosalind, so that she can test his integrity. Finally, news comes to the exiled Duke that his brother has experienced a religious conversion, and the estate has reverted to him. Rosalind reveals her identity and marries Orlando, Celia marries his repentant brother Oliver, and they all return to the court.

As You Like It is partly inspired by *Rosalynde*, a romance by Thomas Lodge, published in 1590, though Shakespeare changed the original French setting to a romanticized version of the Forest of Arden in Warwickshire. It is likely that the play was written in 1599 (it was entered into the Stationer's Register in 1600) and some scholars believe it to be one of the first plays performed at the Globe Theatre on Bankside. It is classed as a comedy in the First Folio.[1] Shakespeare himself is thought to have played the part of Adam. Since women were not permitted on stage in Shakespeare's lifetime, all characters in the play would originally have been performed by male actors.

ROSALIND is the biggest part given to a female character in all of Shakespeare's plays. (It has been suggested that Shakespeare wrote the parts of both Rosalind and Celia for a particularly talented pair of boy actors in his company, The Chamberlain's Men.[2]) She is clever, witty, mischievous and good at acting; before she has even met Orlando, she has been meditating on the concept of romantic love. She is also 'more than common tall', which helps her in her disguise as a boy. Her male outfit features a 'curtal-axe' and a 'boar-spear' as well as doublet and hose. But this manly identity cannot completely obscure her 'woman's fear', nor her vulnerability to the pain and anxiety of being hopelessly in love and unsure of reciprocation. Ganymede – the name she chooses for her male persona – is a beautiful boy in Greek mythology, abducted by Zeus.

If we are to believe her father, CELIA is perhaps the less attractive of the two cousins (though both are described as fair), but she is definitely Rosalind's equal in witty repartee. In her disguise as Aliena, she wears shabby clothes and face paint to make her skin look sunburned. She is certainly more down-to-earth than Rosalind and mocks her friend's irrationality, as she first berates and then defends Orlando. She also inspires loyalty from Touchstone, the court jester who follows the two cousins into exile for the sake of her friendship, and she wins a second father in the shape of Duke Senior.

ROSALIND ON CELIA

I will forget the condition of my estate to rejoice in yours.

CELIA ON ROSALIND

I cannot live out of her company.

'ALL THE WORLD'S A STAGE, and all the men and women merely players', says Jaques, in his famous speech to Duke Senior and his band of outlaws, halfway through the play.[3] The audience, at this point, has been watching Rosalind and Celia pretending to be Ganymede and Aliena as they navigate the potential perils of the Forest of Arden. But, although both must adopt different identities in order to escape the wrath of Duke Frederick, it is their loyalty to one another as friends which helps to bring them back to their fundamental selves at key points in the drama.

Rosalind and Celia are cousins. In the opening act we learn that Rosalind was allowed to stay at court when her father, Duke Senior, was exiled to the Forest because of her close bond with Celia ('being ever from their cradles bred together … never two ladies loved as they do'[4]). But she misses her father and is conflicted over divided loyalties. At the start the cousins are equals in intellect, wit and status, and Celia is keen to compensate for her father's actions: 'for what he hath taken away from thy father perforce, I will render thee again in affection'.[5] They have enormous fun feeding each other punchlines as they joke with Touchstone, the court jester, and they tease the servant who comes to tell them a wrestling match is not suitable entertainment for ladies, already calling into question stereotypical gender identity. They also both root for Orlando in his fight against the reigning champion. Celia sees immediately that Rosalind has fallen for Orlando and encourages her to confess, even though it makes her own situation difficult:

> CELIA ... let us talk in good earnest. Is it possible on such a sudden you should fall into so strong a liking with old Sir Rowland's youngest son?
>
> ROSALIND The Duke my father loved his father dearly.
>
> CELIA Doth it therefore ensue that you should love his son dearly? By this kind of chase I should hate him, for my father hated his father dearly; yet I hate not Orlando.
>
> ROSALIND No, faith, hate him not, for my sake.[6]

Celia is alert to the conventions of court and calls Rosalind away when she throws caution to the wind and makes a suggestive comment to Orlando, telling him he has 'overthrown / More than your enemies'.[7] But when the scene turns from entertainment to political threat, Celia's loyalty is with her friend, not her father, whom she petitions with a passionate speech:

> If she be a traitor,
> Why, so am I. We still have slept together,
> Rose at an instant, learned, played, eat together,
> And wheresoe'er we went, like Juno's swans
> Still we went coupled and inseparable.[8]

The image of the swans – who drew Venus's chariot together – shows how very close the two young women are and how Celia's sense of self is bound up in her relationship with her female cousin, not her father.⁹ Celia ignores her father's attempt to turn their friendship into rivalry ('thou wilt show more bright and seem more virtuous / When she is gone'¹⁰). Instead she goes into voluntary exile with her friend, sharing her misfortune and abandoning her father's inheritance. Turning to Rosalind, she says:

> ... be not thou more grieved than I am ...
> And do not seek to take your change upon you,
> To bear your griefs yourself, and leave me out.
> For by this heaven, now at our sorrows pale,
> Say what thou canst, I'll go along with thee.¹¹

Celia is powerless to change her father's mind, or reverse Rosalind's misfortune, but the one thing she can do is stay with her, come what may.

It is Celia's idea to go in disguise to the Forest of Arden to find Rosalind's father, and in her optimism she regards their exile as an opportunity: 'Now go we in content, / To liberty, and not to banishment.'¹² But once they are settled in the Forest, Rosalind's wooing of Orlando (who thinks she is the male youth Ganymede, pretending to be his idea of Rosalind) takes centre stage. Celia looks on, aligning herself with the audience, encouraging our amusement at Rosalind's reckless deception and teasing her, too, when she pretends not to realize that the bad poetry addressed to her and posted on the trees is by Orlando:

> CELIA Trow you who hath done this?
> ROSALIND Is it a man?¹³

Rosalind's line here is bound to draw a laugh, first because it is disingenuous, and second because this part would originally have been played by a boy, enacting the character of a woman who is disguised as a man. She is so desperate to have Orlando's identity confirmed that she doesn't let Celia get a word in edgeways:

> Alas the day, what shall I do with my doublet and hose! What did he when thou sawest him? What said he? How looked he? Wherein went he? What makes he here? Did he ask for me? Where remains he? How parted he with thee? And when shalt thou see him again? Answer me in one word.[14]

In the end Celia, like all good friends are sometimes obliged to do, tells her to shut up: 'Cry "holla" to thy tongue, I prithee…'[15]

Their tête-à-têtes in the Forest bring Rosalind down to earth and remind her (and us) of her original identity. Indeed, much of the sexual frisson and the funniest moments of the play pivot on ideas of cross-gender and both women exploit these not only by emphasizing gender stereotypes but also undermining them. After her first encounter with Orlando in her disguise as Ganymede, Rosalind says to Celia: 'Never talk to me. I will weep.' Celia's reply reminds her of the expectations prompted by her male outfit: 'Do, I prithee, but yet have the grace to consider that tears do not become a man.'[16] Celia mocks Orlando for writing poetry, hinting, by overuse of the word 'brave', that this is an unmanly activity ('He writes brave verses, speaks brave words, swears brave oaths, and breaks them bravely'[17]). She is unimpressed by Rosalind's testing role-play as a jealous and unfaithful woman, and she interjects to remind Orlando (and Rosalind too) of the true nature of the person he fell in love with: 'he hath a Rosalind of a better leer than you.'[18] Rosalind ignores the brakes Celia is trying to apply, however, and by the end of this scene Celia exclaims 'You have simply misused our sex in your love-prate'[19] and threatens to strip off Rosalind's doublet and hose to expose her sex (which of course would in reality have been male).

Rosalind's comical explorations and subversions of the way men and women are thought to behave in love, and her affectionate exertion of control over Orlando (well nigh impossible, in Elizabethan times, without the male disguise), perhaps explain how Celia comes to fall in love so quickly with Oliver. The cousins are so close ('thou and I am one', Celia says) that she can almost adopt the courtship she has witnessed and transfer it to Orlando's brother. Mirroring this idea, Celia's marriage plans are the catalyst for Rosalind to accept that she now trusts Orlando enough to reveal her identity, though she has one last chance to subvert gender stereotypes by speaking the epilogue of the play (a role traditionally reserved for a male character): 'If I were a woman I would kiss as many of you as had beards that pleased me…'.

At the end of the play, no fewer than four couples get married. Though she has lost a father, Celia has gained an uncle, Duke Senior, who is willing to take his place, and a lover of her own. Both Celia and Rosalind take on new identities as wives and secure their loyal and intimate friendship by becoming sisters-in-law.

Reserve and Recklessness

JANE & EMMA

Emma by Jane Austen

Twenty-one-year-old Emma Woodhouse believes she has a talent for matchmaking among her small social circle in the village of Highbury in Surrey. When Jane Fairfax unexpectedly comes to the village for a protracted visit, Emma thinks she has guessed the reason. After a series of excruciating misunderstandings, she comes to realize that interference in matters of the heart rarely goes well, and she narrowly misses sacrificing her own chance of happiness through her obsession with making matches for everyone else.

According to her sister Cassandra, JANE AUSTEN (1775–1817) started work on *Emma* in 1814. By this time she was living in the cottage at Chawton in Hampshire (now a museum) with her sister, mother and their companion, Martha Lloyd. *Emma* was published in 1815, the fourth and last of her novels to appear in her lifetime. According to Jane's nephew, James Edward Austen-Leigh, she described Emma as 'a heroine whom no-one but myself will much like'.[20] Although Austen recorded that contemporary readers preferred *Pride and Prejudice*, many modern critics see *Emma* as her masterpiece.

EMMA WOODHOUSE is 'handsome, clever and rich'. She has hazel eyes, 'a bloom of full health', an 'open countenance', 'regular features' and a 'happy disposition'. Emma is also of a 'pretty height and size' and she is good at dancing.[21] Emma's robust health and general fitness (she frequently walks into the village or over to her friend Mrs Weston's house) give her a great deal of independence in the limited society in which she lives. Although only five years old when she lost her mother, she has been well looked after by her governess, who, at the start of the novel, has left the family home and married a neighbour, Mr Weston.

JANE FAIRFAX is also twenty-one years old. She has grey eyes and dark eyelashes, dark hair and an unusual complexion ('not regular, but … very pleasing', according to Emma) which is also admired for its 'bloom'.[22] She is most often described as elegant and graceful, but she is also reserved, and unwilling to express her opinion in society. Jane is a talented pianist. Like Emma, she is the ideal height and weight. Her health, however, is often in question. Jane is an orphan who has been taken in by a moderately well-off family, the Campbells. But now that her stepsister has married she can no longer live with the family long-term, and must support herself by becoming a governess.

JANE ON EMMA

I know what my manners were to you. – So cold and artificial! – I had always a part to act. – It was a life of deceit! – I know that I must have disgusted you.

EMMA ON JANE
I wish Jane Fairfax very well,
but she tires me to death.

T HE FEMALE FRIENDSHIPS in Jane Austen's novels are
rarely straightforward: in *Pride and Prejudice* Elizabeth
Bennet's best friend Charlotte Lucas agrees to marry Elizabeth's obsequious cousin Mr Collins just days after he proposed
to Elizabeth; Catherine Morland's friend Isabella Thorpe
leads her astray in *Northanger Abbey*; and sisters Elinor and
Marianne are manipulated by the duplicitous Lucy Steele in
Sense and Sensibility. But the friendships in *Emma* have an added
complexity. Emma is the only heroine in Jane Austen's novels
to have independent wealth and therefore a comparatively large
degree of control over her social life. In addition, although
most of the novel is narrated to us from Emma's perspective,
it is not until the end of the book that we realize how flawed
her judgement is. As many critics have pointed out, it takes at
least a second reading of the novel to appreciate the levels of
irony at work. On a first reading, many readers are likely to
side with Emma in her dislike of Jane Fairfax at the start of the
novel; on a second reading, the scales tip in the other direction.

From the start, Austen is keen to emphasize the similarities
between the two women. They are both twenty-one, they are
both well-educated and accomplished, they are both handsome.
Their situations are also carefully mirrored: both are reacting to
a change of personal circumstance brought about by a marriage.

Both also, for a short time, are attracted to the same man (Frank Churchill, Mr Weston's son from a former marriage). But Emma, perhaps because her family and Jane's family have encouraged it so much, has stubbornly refused to actively develop her acquaintance with Jane, rather like a young child who is too self-conscious to play with another just because their parents would find it convenient for them to get on:

> Why she did not like Jane Fairfax might be a difficult question to answer; Mr Knightley had once told her it was because she saw in her the really accomplished young woman, which she wanted to be thought herself; and though the accusation had been eagerly refuted at the time, there were moments of self-examination in which her conscience could not quite acquit her. But 'she could never get acquainted with her; she did not know how it was, but there was such coldness and reserve ... and it had been always imagined that they were to be so intimate – because their ages were the same, every body had supposed they must be so fond of each other.' These were her reasons – she had no better.[23]

Everyone remarks on Jane's superior piano-playing, and over the years Emma has had to endure Jane's loquacious aunt, Miss Bates, extolling Jane's virtues and reading out loud from her letters. As Mr Knightley hints, there is no small amount of jealousy there.

Although Emma has the best intentions, on meeting her again, to revive her friendship with Jane (her equal, or even superior, in accomplishment), she chooses instead to nurture a new friend in Harriet Smith, very much inferior to Emma in intellect, education and (in the terms of the novel) social standing, being illegitimate and currently living at a boarding school. Harriet poses no threat to Emma's sense of self-worth. Emma also maintains her lifelong friendship with Mrs Weston, who, even during her years as Emma's governess, has allowed her to do 'just what she liked'.[24]

In Emma's defence, it is Jane Fairfax's reserve which proves the stumbling block and undoes Emma's good intentions. 'There was no getting at her real opinion. Wrapt up in a cloak of politeness, she seemed determined to hazard nothing. She was disgustingly, was suspiciously reserved', Emma observes, after an evening spent in the company of Jane and her relatives.[25] It is only on a second reading that we have sympathy for this reserve, necessary to conceal Jane's secret engagement to Frank Churchill without telling outright lies to her Highbury friends. In her reticence, Jane is, in fact, protecting her friendship with Emma. But Emma sees it as a continuation of a trait she has always disliked, and she boasts to Frank: 'I must be more in want of a friend, or an agreeable companion, than I have yet been, to take the trouble of conquering any body's reserve to procure one.'[26]

For the purposes of the plot, Emma and Jane cannot be intimate friends, because the story turns on the confusions and misunderstandings caused by Jane's secret. Emma's inability to pick up any of the clues about this situation leads her to flirt recklessly with Frank, spread a rumour about Jane being secretly in love with her stepsister's husband and behave ungraciously towards Jane's aunt. No one could accuse Emma of being too reserved.

As the novel progresses, however, the two women inch closer towards a mutual understanding. Aware that her behaviour with Frank is below par, Emma does her best to hold herself in check at future social events and tries not to respond to his teasing. In a welcome moment of vulnerability, Jane seeks Emma's help when she wishes to escape from the awkward strawberry-picking party at which Frank Churchill has failed to appear:

> 'Miss Woodhouse, we all know at times what it is to be wearied in spirits. Mine, I confess, are exhausted. The greatest kindness you can shew me, will be to let me have my own way, and only say that I am gone when it is necessary.'

Emma can now find some rapport with Jane, empathizing with her fatigue, and pitying her for having to endure life with Miss Bates. At last there is a degree of intimacy on which a possible friendship can be founded. After offering her help, she watches her 'safely off with the zeal of a friend'.[27]

Even so, Emma has further blunders to make before she realizes the full extent of her misunderstanding of Jane's situation. When Jane and Frank's engagement is temporarily broken off after the notoriously awful Box Hill picnic, Jane accepts a position as governess, arranged by the unspeakably snobbish and interfering Mrs Elton, and promptly becomes ill. Emma tries her best to be a friend at this point, inviting her to her home, or out for a drive in her carriage, and sending her arrowroot as a remedy. But everything is formally declined, and Emma sees that her attempts at friendship have been tardy and inadequate: 'She bitterly regretted not having sought a closer acquaintance with her, and blushed for the envious feelings which had certainly been, in some measure, the cause.'[28]

It is not until the secret engagement is restored and revealed that Emma and Jane can have a chance at friendship. The inadequate reactions of Emma's friends Harriet Smith and Mrs Weston are also telling at this point. Harriet confesses her ridiculous crush on Mr Knightley (and Emma at last sees that she has been irresponsible in encouraging Harriet to be overambitious in finding a husband), and Mrs Weston defends Frank, who Emma now sees has behaved abominably.

It is interesting that soon after she learns of Jane's engagement, Emma herself becomes engaged to Mr Knightley, so once again her and Jane's situations are mirrored, and now, through Jane's marriage to Frank, they will be closer in financial terms. Emma calls on Jane once she knows the full story, but finds Mrs Elton is already in the Bates's parlour, revelling in the false idea that she alone knows the secret. Why does Austen not write a scene in which Jane and Emma are alone together, when Jane can finally drop her reserve and resurrect the friendship? Perhaps she couldn't resist poking fun at Mrs Elton one last time, perhaps she wanted us to like Emma more than Jane, or she felt that a sudden reconciliation, after so much jealousy and suspicion, would simply not be realistic. Instead, Jane and Emma convey their feelings through actions, as if neither can now trust speech to be sincere. As she greets Emma at the door, after several stuttering false starts, Jane says 'excuse me for being so entirely without words'. In the sitting room, Jane 'was wanting to give her words, not to Mrs Elton, but to Miss

Woodhouse, as the latter plainly saw … though it could not often proceed beyond a look'. And Emma has at last learnt discretion, conveying her feelings to Jane via 'a very, very earnest shake of the hand'. They only have time for a snatched series of apologies on the stairs as Emma leaves, which Emma concludes by saying: 'Pray say no more. I feel that all the apologies should be on my side. Let us forgive each other at once.'[29]

But is Austen setting up a future friendship for Jane and Emma, beyond the end of the novel? With all traces of jealousy diffused and laughed at, it is tempting to believe that their relationship will flourish. However, Austen is not clear if Jane and Frank are part of the 'small band of true friends' at Emma's wedding to Mr Knightley (it is hard to imagine Mr Knightley overcoming his disapproval and welcoming Frank to Donwell Abbey), or indeed if Emma and Mr Knightley will attend their wedding at Enscombe. Perhaps any such friendship is destined to be short-lived: according to family anecdote, Austen often described the afterlives of her characters, and tradition had it that Jane would only survive for another nine or ten years.[30] But in the terms of the novel, Austen leaves it to us to decide whether, having started off so disastrously on the wrong foot, Emma will now pursue one last chance at friendship with her elegant and accomplished peer.

Light and Shade

LUCY & MAGGIE

The Mill on the Floss by George Eliot

The story of Maggie Tulliver's childhood at Dorlcote Mill in the town of St Ogg's, the novel follows her progress to early adulthood in rural Warwickshire in the 1820s to 30s. Maggie, along with her older brother Tom, must learn to adapt to their father's bankruptcy (a result of a vendetta with a local lawyer, old Wakem). In doing so, she struggles to navigate the restrictions of Victorian provincial life, with tragic consequences.

GEORGE ELIOT (Mary Ann Evans, 1819–1880) finished *The Mill on the Floss* in 1860. By this time she was living with George Lewes, but they could not marry because Lewes was not able to divorce his estranged wife (by now living with another man). It was the beginning of a decade of movement towards social change: the first petition for mass votes for women was launched in 1866, the Second Reform Act was passed in 1867, and the provision of education for the less wealthy increased. Eliot drew on her memories of a childhood in Chilvers Coton near Nuneaton, Warwickshire, for the milieu of the novel, including her brother Isaac (who disowned her when she began her relationship with Lewes). Within months of publication, the first print run had sold out.

MAGGIE TULLIVER is tall, dark, tempestuous and clever. Even at the age of nine her father thinks she is 'Too [a]'cute for a woman'.[31] She is smarter than her brother Tom and envious of his schooling, much preferring reading and daydreaming to needlework. Maggie's mother is frustrated by her clumsiness and her ability to get her clothes dirty, but the scruffy girl with 'Medusa' hair grows into a woman of unusual beauty, and by the time she is seventeen 'the eyes are liquid, the brown cheek is firm and rounded, the full lips are red'.[32] Her childhood sweetheart Philip Wakem finds her 'as open and transparent as a rock-pool',[33] while her cousin Lucy's suitor, Stephen Guest, is drawn to her because she is 'full of delicious opposites'.[34]

LUCY DEANE is petite, blonde and obedient: 'everything about her was neat – her little round neck with the row of coral beads, her little straight nose ... her little clear eyebrows, rather darker than her curls, to match her hazel eyes.'[35] As a child she does what she is told, though she does 'timidly enjoy' straying beyond the boundary of her Aunt Pullet's garden with Tom and Maggie. She loves animals and owns a dog, a horse and several canaries. She is at boarding school with Maggie, but she doesn't have Maggie's passion for books, though they both have a love of music. In adult life she is a pretty and competent hostess, adept at bringing people together via benign 'little plots' to improve their lives. Everyone views her as benevolent, but her ability to see only the good in people lets her down as the relationships of her friends become more complex.

LUCY ON MAGGIE

There is no girl in the world I love
so well as my cousin Maggie.

MAGGIE ON LUCY

You dear tiny thing ... you enjoy other people's
happiness so much, I believe you would do without
any of your own. I wish I were like you.

M AGGIE TULLIVER is an extraordinary literary heroine.
A fascinating mix of passionate contradictions, she
has caught the imagination and inspired the empathy of many
readers over the century and a half since *The Mill on the Floss*
was published. Those who identify with her right from the start
of the novel, when she cuts off her hair in a fit of temper, runs
away to join the so-called Gypsies and incurs the wrath of her
imperious aunts, might also be inclined, out of loyalty to their
heroine, to rather dislike her cousin and friend Lucy Deane,
with her neat golden curls, who never puts a foot wrong, who
might seem, at first, so perfect as to be rather insufferable.

Indeed, George Eliot is at pains to emphasize their physical
differences, a literary device used not long before by Walter
Scott in his bestselling novel *Waverley*, published in 1814.
Like Scott's character, the passionate and rebellious Flora
Mac-Ivor, Maggie is dark, and, like placid and domesticated
Rose Brawardine, Lucy is fair. Maggie is compared to dogs – a
skye terrier or an unruly puppy – while Lucy is a white kitten,
a little puss, a mouse. Lucy wears her fine clothes naturally
and gracefully; Maggie is constantly pulling at her collar or
removing her bonnet. Maggie will be tall; Lucy is always
described as 'little'.

But Eliot is also clear that Maggie adores Lucy. She loves to admire her prettiness, and, aged nine, she begs her aunts and mother to let her cousin stay the night at Dorlcote Mill. Even when she pushes Lucy into the mud at the pond outside her Aunt Pullet's house it is clear that this is an outlet for her anger towards vindictive brother Tom, not Lucy herself. Lucy, in turn, tries to mediate between Maggie and Tom so that Maggie will be encouraged to recount to her the imaginative tales she loves to hear. So, although Lucy and Maggie are set up to be compared and perhaps to compare themselves with each other, there is never any jealousy between them.

This is what makes Maggie's dilemma, in book 6 of the novel, especially poignant. Now seventeen, Maggie has endured the consequences of her father's bankruptcy and his premature death. Her beloved books have been sold, she has had to leave boarding school early, and to maintain her independence from the tyrannous aunts she is earning a living as a teacher. She is staying with Lucy for a brief respite before taking up another teaching position. Lucy delights in looking after her cousin and soon confides that she is in love with Stephen Guest, a frequent visitor to the Deane household. Maggie jokes with her about withholding approval – 'I shall be very difficult to please... A gentleman who thinks he is good enough for Lucy, must expect to be sharply criticised',[36] – but when Stephen and Maggie meet, there is an unexpected frisson of attraction between them which becomes irresistible: 'Each was oppressively conscious of the other's presence, even

to the finger-ends. Yet each looked and longed for the same
thing to happen the next day.'[37]

As they inevitably see more of each other at Lucy's house,
Maggie is undoubtedly pursued by Stephen. But although she
remains passive in response to his advances towards her, she
is also moved by them, and excited by the secretive nature of
it all, as his subtle flirtations are made in full view of Lucy:

> That tone of gentle solicitude obliged her to look at the
> face that was bent towards her and to say, 'No, thank
> you' – and once looking nothing could prevent that mutual
> glance from being delicious to both, as it had been the
> evening before.[38]

By this time, Maggie's former sweetheart, young Philip
Wakem, is back on the scene, but she doesn't seek refuge in
that relationship either (partly because of their fathers' dispute
and Tom's disapproval). Instead, she wavers, allows Stephen to
kiss her, and then sends him away:

> There were moments in which a cruel selfishness seemed
> to be getting possession of her: why should not Lucy – why
> should not Philip suffer? *She* had had to suffer through many
> years of her life, and who had renounced anything for her?

But then again:

> She might as well hope to enjoy walking by maiming her feet,
> as hope to enjoy an existence in which she set out by maiming
> the faith and sympathy that were the best organs of her soul.[39]

We see this from Maggie's perspective (Lucy is happily
oblivious to her suitor's games) – and understand how she is

trying desperately not to betray her friend, yet her inexplicable desire for Stephen is pushing her further and further towards it.

A series of twists of fate tip Maggie over the point of no return when, through no fault of her own, she ends up alone with Stephen on a boating trip. Stephen immediately takes advantage and rows far down the river until it is too late for them to return with the tide. They are taken up by a steamer and Maggie spends the night on the deck of the boat without a chaperone – an act of unforgiveable impropriety in the eyes of Victorian society.

Although Maggie ultimately rejects Stephen in order to preserve her friendships with Lucy and Philip, she does so too late. The damage is done, and by the time she returns to St Ogg's gossip is rife; she is ostracized by her brother Tom, who evicts both her and her mother from the mill, and Lucy becomes ill and takes to her bed. Maggie is too distressed at the hurt she has caused to take up her teaching position away from St Ogg's, but also desperate for independence: 'I must get my own bread',[40] she tells her mother. This impulse is perhaps ultimately behind her rejection of both Stephen and Philip. At one point she tells Philip: 'I begin to think there can never come much happiness to me from loving: I have always had so much pain mingled with it. I wish I could make myself a world outside it, as men do.'[41]

The desire for a 'world outside' domestic relationships also shows us how Lucy and Maggie (like Scott's Rose and Flora) represent different female roles within the story. Lucy – less bookish than Maggie – has more emotional intelligence and an understanding of how to influence society without pushing at the boundaries of etiquette. Having persuaded her father to help restore Dorlcote Mill to Tom and Maggie through his professional connections, she boasts: 'I'm very wise – I've got all your business talents'.[42] But Maggie, though experienced on the subjects of Euclid, Thomas à Kempis and Logic, with a good knowledge of Latin, is too honest for small talk, and 'had never in her life spoken from the lips merely, so that she must necessarily appear absurd to more experienced ladies'.[43]

After the incident with Stephen, etiquette forbids Maggie from visiting Lucy, though she is haunted by 'a face that had been turned on hers with glad sweet looks of trust and love from the twilight time of memory: changed now to a sad and weary face by a first heart-stroke'.[44] It falls to Lucy to orchestrate a reconciliation with her cousin, in what is the most courageous and affecting act of friendship in the book. Using her talent for avoiding confrontation (since her father would have forbidden her to see Maggie) she sneaks out and finds Maggie in her lodgings by the river. Before they can speak, Lucy embraces Maggie and puts her face against her cheek in an act of childlike affection. This gives Maggie the courage to apologize and Lucy immediately forgives her: 'It is a trouble that has come on us all; you have more to bear than I have.'[45] Lucy explains she is going away for the sake of her health, but she is sure that on her return they can become friends again, confident of her ability to bring her family round. Their bond of friendship will transcend their very different attitudes to life and to men.

But it is too late. Maggie is now set on a collision course with the values and prejudices of the majority of St Ogg's, who want her to leave town. This is the tragic metaphor at the finale of the book, as the river floods catastrophically and Maggie is borne away on the tide, rushed downriver too fast on her little boat. She manages to rescue Tom from the mill, but on their way to find Lucy they are both drowned when the boat is dashed to pieces on the large obstacle of detritus from the ruined barns and houses blocking the way in midstream.

Is Eliot punishing Maggie for being too clever, too independent, and not the blonde, marriageable stereotype represented by her cousin Lucy? If that were the case, surely Lucy would condemn her too. But in the conclusion to the book we learn that 'years after' a man visits Maggie's tombstone with a 'sweet face' beside him, and this can only be Stephen and Lucy, eventually able to resume their relationship after slow progression towards reconciliation, but never forgetting their friend Maggie Tulliver, the girl who lived out of her time and suffered the consequences.

Three Cheers for the Singletons

BRIDGET, JUDE, SHAZZER & TOM

Bridget Jones's Diary & Bridget Jones:
The Edge of Reason by Helen Fielding

The first two books in the Bridget Jones series relate the rare triumphs and comical mishaps of a single thirty-something woman working in the media in London in the 1990s.

Bridget Jones's Diary first appeared in 1995 as a satirical column in the *Independent*. An editor at the paper wanted Helen Fielding to write a column about her personal life as a single professional woman, but she was concerned that this would be too exposing, so they agreed that instead she should write in the voice of a fictional character. This freed her up to be heart-warmingly honest about the difference between the 'veneer' of a professional woman in her thirties and 'what's going on inside', which in turn won her a large and loyal following and sparked a whole new genre in commercial fiction: so-called 'chick lit'.[46] Though Fielding has expressed shock, looking back, at the amount of sexism Bridget faces, she has also described her delight that new generations of readers still empathize with Bridget because 'it really is about the way we relate to our friends'.[47] Fielding's own close friends, journalist and presenter Tracey MacLeod and film director Sharon Maguire, partly inspired the characters of Jude and Sharon in the books.

BRIDGET grew up in Grafton Underwood in Northamptonshire. Though we are given a daily update on her weight (something Helen Fielding used to note down in her own diaries when she was a student), there is in fact no physical description of Bridget in the book, so we do not know whether her dissatisfaction with her appearance is justified or not. We do know, however, that she weighs somewhere between 8.5 and 9.5 stone, depending on her intake of chocolate croissants. Bridget is addicted to Silk Cut, chardonnay, Bloody Marys, Milk Tray, lottery scratch cards and the BBC's adaptation of *Pride and Prejudice*. She at first works in publishing and then for *Sit Up Britain*, a daytime television programme.

JUDE is Head of Futures at Brightlings in the City. Her boyfriend is the commitment-phobe Vile Richard, partially responsible for her library of self-help books, on which she is an expert. Jude gets up at 5.45 a.m. every day to go to the gym before starting work at 8.30 a.m. ('mad', as Bridget points out). She is tall and thin, and when she is upset she sounds like a sheep.

SHARON (SHAZZER) works in IT (by the third book she is a dotcom whizz in Silicon Valley). She coins the phrase 'emotional fuckwittage' and also reclaims the word 'singleton' (originally used in this way by P.G. Wodehouse) as a positive description of anyone not in a couple. She has a low, guttural voice, growls when she is cross, and is formidable in political/gender debates (or feminist rants).

TOM is in an on–off relationship with Pretentious Jerome. Like Bridget, he is dissatisfied with his personal appearance, especially his nose. He is an expert on telephone techniques, specifically how to disguise obsessive calling to a potential boyfriend's answerphone. Having grown up in the 1970s, Bridget and Tom are especially close: 'Tom has a theory that homosexuals and single women in their thirties have natural bonding: both being accustomed to disappointing their parents and being treated as freaks by society.'[48] He becomes a psychologist.

H ELEN FIELDING famously stole the romantic plot for *Bridget Jones's Diary* from *Pride and Prejudice*, but this is a story not so much about finding Mr Right as about celebrating the importance of your true friends. As Tom points out in *The Edge of Reason*, 'if Miss Havisham had had some jolly flatmates to take the piss out of her she would never have stayed so long in her wedding dress.'[49]

Tom and the joyously original characters of Bridget, Shazzer and Jude have many things in common. In their early thirties, they are single and living in London, and all, on occasion, fear a lonely death, being found 'half-eaten by an Alsatian'. But most importantly (and hilariously), they are endlessly baffled, wrong-footed and disappointed by the confusing world of dating in the late twentieth century, and constantly juggling the demands of career, social life (including cooking gourmet dinners for eight) and living up to a standard of personal appearance sold to them by lifestyle magazines. As Bridget confesses in her diary while she prepares for a date:

> Wise people will say Daniel should like me just as I am, but I am a child of *Cosmopolitan* culture, have been traumatized by supermodels and too many quizzes and know that neither my personality nor my body is up to it if left to its own devices.[50]

According to Sharon, a lot of this angst can be put down to 'fuckwittage' on the part of ruthless, commitment-shy single men and she gloriously sums up their situation in full feminist-rant mode at an emergency summit to discuss Jude's Vile Richard in Café Rouge:

> We women are only vulnerable because we are a pioneer
> generation daring to refuse to compromise in love and
> relying on our own economic power. In twenty years' time
> men won't even dare start with fuckwittage because we will
> just *laugh in their faces...*[51]

In fact, it is thanks to Sharon's analysis that Bridget initially manages not to sleep with her boss, Daniel Cleaver. Later, after she *has* slept with him, she detects a lie and momentarily saves herself from further humiliation by remembering her friend's advice: 'A siren blared in my head and a huge neon sign started flashing with Sharon's head in the middle going, "FUCKWITTAGE, FUCKWITTAGE".'[52]

Advice from the friends, though well-intentioned and highly addictive, is not always consistent or straightforward. Jude tries to look at relationships through analyses along the lines of self-help book *Men are from Mars, Women are from Venus*, Sharon congratulates Bridget for being strong, while Tom guesses her true feelings:

> It was good ringing up Sharon to boast about being Mrs
> Iron Knickers but when I rang Tom he saw straight through
> it and said, 'Oh, my poor darling,' which made me go silent
> trying not to burst into self-pitying tears.[53]

Nevertheless, the irony is (and at the time this was an unusual angle in commercial fiction, which didn't represent the growing numbers of professional single women) that the friends know each other so well that they have in fact developed their own support network which liberates them from reliance on a man. When Tom, recovering from cosmetic surgery, is dumped by Pretentious Jerome and hides in his flat for a weekend thinking nobody loves him, Bridget tells him to listen to her answerphone, 'which held twenty-two frantic messages from his friends, all distraught because he had disappeared for twenty-four hours, which put paid to all our fears about dying alone and being eaten by an Alsatian'.[54] It is Jude and Shazzer who meet Bridget at Heathrow after her spell in a Thai jail, rescue her from the media scrum and stock her flat with pizza, chocolate and chardonnay. When Bridget decides to cook dinner for the friends on her birthday, they know, from past subjection to culinary disasters, that they should secretly book a restaurant and take her out instead as a surprise. At another dinner party, designed to impress Mark Darcy, when Bridget accidentally makes blue soup and forgets the ingredients for the main course, Tom creatively suggests they should abandon Grand Marnier Crème Anglaise for dessert and 'merely drink Grand Marnier'.[55]

Mark Darcy (Mr Right), however, is not put off by Bridget's cooking so much as her friends and their constant telephone calls. He is prone to smacking himself on the forehead whenever she picks up the handset. But as she explains, 'The thing is, Jude and Shaz have been kind to me for years before I even met Mark so obviously it would not be right to leave the answerphone on now.'[56] With or without a boyfriend, she is just as reliant on them, to the extent that she wishes she could ring them up for advice in the middle of an intimidating Law Society Dinner she attends as Mark's date.

Misunderstandings ensue in the second book, and it's not long before Mark and Bridget split up, bringing the friends back to centre stage (when treacherous 'frenemy' Rebecca temporarily steals Mark, they immediately come around with ice cream, cigarettes and the *Pride and Prejudice* DVD). In this way, there is a dramatic tension throughout the diaries, in that, though we empathize with Bridget and want her to find love, the writing and dialogue are far funnier when she doesn't (no surprise, then, that in the third book, *Mad About the Boy*, Bridget is already a widow and Jude a divorcee). Bridget herself guiltily voices this paradox when she tries to meet up with Tom and discovers he is going on a date: 'Oh God, I hate it when Tom is happy, confident and getting on well with Jerome, much preferring it when he is miserable, insecure and neurotic.'[57]

Sharon has the best lines for 'smug married' couples who ask Bridget when she is going to find a husband and start having children and surely speaks for many when she supportively rants: 'You should have said "I'm not married because I'm a *Singleton*, you smug, prematurely ageing, narrow-minded morons"',[58] and Tom's analyses of contemporary relationships are spot on: 'I know we're all psychotic, single and completely dysfunctional and it's all done over the phone … but it's a bit like a family, isn't it?'[59]

The best friends denounce your boyfriend from the rooftops when he dumps you but are ultimately willing to be a brides-maid at your wedding when you foolishly marry him. And, in fact, it is Jude who, in a speech at her controversial marriage to Vile Richard, pays the most heartfelt tribute to a friendship that will fundamentally endure through the years as boyfriends and husbands come and go: 'I promise … to keep in constant contact with my best friends, Bridget and Sharon, who are living proof that the Urban Singleton Family is just as strong and supportive, just as there for you, as anyone's blood family.'[60]

Adventure

'FREEDOM, SANCHO, is one of the most precious gifts heaven gave to men; the treasures under the earth and beneath the sea cannot compare to it', so says Don Quixote to his loyal friend and servant.[1] Some embark on their journeys in celebration of it, others to defend it, but ultimately many adventurers would agree. The potential of release from everyday routines and overly familiar surroundings tends to give us itchy feet – as when Mole abandons his spring cleaning and makes a run for it, or Frodo strays further and further from the Shire, or Holmes sets out from the bohemian comforts of 221B Baker Street. Each protagonist needs a loyal friend as a foil to the quirks of his own character, someone who may be reluctant at first to join in, but ultimately commits to the quest and proves crucial to its success. (Tolkien reverses this trope by making Frodo the reluctant hero and Sam his much more enthusiastic companion.) Indeed, Sam and Sancho bring wisdom beyond their roles, and transform these relationships into unforgettable friendships, bound together forever by sharing the terrors and triumphs of unpredictable adventures.

Bickering and Bonhomie

DON QUIXOTE &
SANCHO PANZA

The Ingenious Gentleman Don Quixote of
La Mancha by Miguel de Cervantes

Don Quixote, a self-proclaimed knight-errant, and Sancho
Panza, his make-believe squire, travel through Spain on a
horse and a donkey, looking for adventures.

By the time he published the first part of his bestselling novel *Don
Quixote*, in 1605, MIGUEL DE CERVANTES (1547–1616) had been
permanently injured in the Battle of Lepanto, captured by pirates,
enslaved in Algiers and imprisoned for fraud: a rather more adventurous life than is usually expected for a writer. In 1614, a rival using the
pseudonym Alonso Fernández de Avellanada wrote an unauthorized
sequel to his bestseller; Cervantes was so incensed by this plagiarism
that he wove it into his own second volume, published a year later.
Don Quixote was reprinted several times in its first year of publication
(a rare first edition of Part I has been housed in the Bodleian Library
since 1605). It is often described as marking the birth of the novel and
has had a huge influence on European literature.[2] The first English
translation appeared in 1612.

DON QUIXOTE is skinny, scrawny and tall with a sallow, long face and hollow cheeks. He has read too many stories of chivalry and romance, leading him to become delusional. Of uncertain name (the narrator explains that the sources vary from Quixada, Quexada or Quexana), he also adopts different sobriquets during his adventures, including The Knight of the Sorrowful Face (because he has lost so many teeth in combat) and The Knight of the Lions. When he is not on adventures, he lives with his niece and housekeeper in a village in La Mancha. He is a great admirer of King Arthur, believes he has the strength and courage of a hundred men, and is in love with Dulcinea of Toboso.

Don Quixote's horse is named ROCINANTE. He is as skinny as his rider, has cracked hooves, is not very fast and falls over a lot. Rocinante sometimes leads the adventure, since Don Quixote lets him go wherever he likes. He is very fond of Sancho's donkey and loyal to Don Quixote, patiently enduring mishaps and injuries.

SANCHO PANZA is a farmer who lives in the same village as Don Quixote: they have known each other since they were babies. He has a family and keeps pigs and a donkey. Rather plump, with an unkempt beard, he loves eating garlic, onions, meat pies and curds, and drinking wine. (He sometimes sits side-saddle on his donkey, rummaging in the pack saddles for food and drink to consume as they travel along.) Unsurprisingly, he is prone to belching. Sancho cannot read or write (though he can sign his name), but he is well-versed in proverbs and very talkative. He is peace-loving and often refuses to fight or runs away when battle commences.

Sancho's donkey is sometimes called DAPPLE or 'the grey'. He is a champion trotter and Sancho praises his comfortable gait. Dapple always returns to Sancho and likes to lean up against Rocinante when they are put to graze. The friendship between horse and donkey is comically compared to the legendary bond between Pylades and Orestes.

DON QUIXOTE ON SANCHO PANZA
Rascally clown, boorish, insolent, and ignorant, ill-spoken,
foul-mouthed, impudent backbiter and slanderer!

SANCHO PANZA ON DON QUIXOTE
Is it possible that your worship is so thick of
skull and so short of brains that you cannot
see that what I say is the simple truth?

W HEN THEY SET OUT on their crazy journey across Spain, looking for adventures at crossroads, forests and wild places, Don Quixote is fifty years old and Sancho Panza is old enough to have a wife and several children, including a daughter of marriageable age. This is therefore not a 'gap year' to gain youthful experience; instead it has all the hallmarks of a major midlife crisis.

Don Quixote's optimistic ambition is to live by the rules of chivalry, engaging in battle with anyone who opposes them, righting wrongs and helping the needy. He is never happier than when embarking on what he perceives as the start of a quest. Sancho's ambition is to become the governor of an ínsula (island), something Don Quixote has promised is a common reward for loyal squires of knights-errant. Much of the brilliance of this book lies in the free-ranging conversations between knight and squire as they travel along on their beloved Rocinante and Dapple, and the gap between what they believe, or say they believe, and reality. In Part I they often discuss how they will achieve fame and fortune. These conversations

are endearingly delusional, each character focused on an unattainable goal and egging the other on:

> 'when I am king I can certainly grant you nobility without
> your buying it or serving me in any way. Because when you are
> made a count, you will find that you are a gentleman, too, and
> ... they will have to call you lord, even if they do not wish to.'
>
> 'And by my faith, I'll know how to carry off that tittle,' said
> Sancho.
>
> 'You mean *title*, not *tittle*,' said his master.
>
> 'Whatever it is,' responded Sancho. '...when I put a duke's
> cape on my back, or dress in gold and pearls ... they'll be
> coming to see me for a hundred leagues around.'
>
> 'You will look fine,' said Don Quixote, 'but it will be
> necessary for you to shave your beard often; yours is so heavy,
> tangled and unkempt that unless you shave with a razor at
> least every other day, people will see what you are from as far
> away as you can shoot a flintlock.'[3]

Through these exchanges, both master and servant represent
aspects of the unattainable ambitions and dreams of ordinary
people, and the fact that however optimistic Don Quixote is
('anything is possible' is a favourite phrase of his) he is doomed
to fail, and that Sancho's dream of governing an island is
ludicrous given that he is illiterate, work-shy and easily taken
in, has gained them sympathy and affection from readers
throughout the centuries.

Notwithstanding their shared ambitions, knight and squire
often disagree about the best course of action. Sancho is
grounded in reality and will only go along with his master's
fantasies to a certain point. Their different perspectives are
often comical:

'Do you not hear the neighing of the horses, the call of the clarions, the sound of the drums?'

'I don't hear anything ... except the bleating of lots of sheep.'[4]

As with any two people who spend every minute of every day (and often much of the night) in each other's company, Sancho and Don Quixote become hyper-aware of each other's flaws, and as the adventure proceeds neither holds back from pointing them out. Don Quixote becomes so annoyed with Sancho's talkativeness that he at one point bans him from speaking, until Sancho complains about this so much that he relents. For his part, Sancho can't stand it when he is about to fall asleep and his master starts to talk about his lady Dulcinea of Toboso, whom neither has ever met. Don Quixote, who is well-read and learned, can't resist pointing out Sancho's grammatical mistakes, and each time he does this Sancho is hurt and offended. As the time they spend in each other's company accumulates, they become more and more frank with each other, so that when Don Quixote offers Sancho a choice of reward – the spoils of their first adventure or alternatively the foals due to be born from the three mares he owns back in the village – Sancho says: 'I'll take the foals ... because it's not very certain that the spoils of your first adventure will be any good.'[5] Later, when Sancho declares he doesn't believe Don Quixote's account of what he saw in the cave of Montesinos, they have this priceless exchange:

'Since I know you, Sancho ... I shall ignore your words.'

'And I won't pay attention to your grace's,' replied Sancho.[6]

They have moments of incandescent anger, and Don Quixote at one point strikes his poor servant for a perceived insult to Dulcinea. In return, Sancho grumbles for the entire length of Part I and some of Part II about the time when Don Quixote abandoned him to be attacked by an unpaid innkeeper. They don't forgive each other so much as put up with each other's shortcomings.

Interspersed with these squabbles, let-downs and fallings-out, however, are the entertaining adventures in which they find themselves: under attack from sheep, unseated from donkey and horse, stuck in trees, poisoned by 'magic' medicine or trampled by pigs. Both often have to drag each other's bruised bodies onto their long-suffering steeds after yet another ill-advised charge.

Despite their disagreements, when Sancho is tricked into believing he has at last been given the governorship of an island, and the pair are separated, Don Quixote misses his squire and Sancho writes to him complaining of the lack of food in his new post. Though, as governor, Sancho makes many wise decisions for his fake citizens, it is not long before he decides to mount his beloved donkey (now bedecked in a silk halter) and return to his knight, 'whose companionship pleased him more than being governor of all the ínsulas in the world'.[7]

Through the course of this mock-heroic novel, both Sancho and Don Quixote journey towards self-recognition and acceptance of their limitations in life. Sancho reaches his destination first:

'I'm not good for governing unless it's a herd of livestock …
the riches you can gain in governorships come at the cost of
your rest and your sleep…'[8]

But for Don Quixote it takes a toppling of both him and
Rocinante at the hands of The Knight of the White Moon
(who is really his neighbour, Samson Carrasco, in disguise)
before he finally accepts that he is not the flower of chivalry, or
The Knight of the Lions, but plain Alonso Quixano, returning
home to die peacefully among friends. To their astonishment,
he rejects the books of chivalry that inspired him to take to
the road and describes them as absurd and deceptive. Instead,
he focuses on finalizing his will in order to ensure that his
loyal friend Sancho Panza is rewarded for his fidelity and
companionship.

In this poignant ending, Cervantes seems to be saying to us,
through his many narrative techniques and his larger-than-life
characters, that it is alright to indulge in fantasies, to charge
and be toppled, to 'tilt at windmills', to accept your limitations
and go home. His warm-hearted narrative of human failings
and disappointments has given his two principal characters
extraordinary fame beyond the bounds of the novel. Cervantes
even works their popularity into the second part of the book,
in which the two friends discuss their portrayal in Part I
(and the plagiarized Part II) and learn of readers' enthusiastic
comments: 'let Don Quixote go charging and Sancho Panza
keep talking, and whatever else happens, that will make
us happy.'[9] Little did the author know that his hero's name

would become an English adjective, *quixotic*, meaning naively idealistic, unrealistic, whimsical.[10]

So, despite Cervantes's warning to imitators at the end – 'For me alone was Don Quixote born' – he didn't succeed in restricting this unforgettable, eccentric and unequal friendship to his seventeenth-century novel. Instead, the pair have journeyed on, delighting readers and inspiring master-and-servant partnerships (Blackadder and Baldrick, Antipholus and Dromio, Jeeves and Wooster, even Frodo and Sam, to name a few) through the years, especially those who find themselves at a midlife crossroads, tempted perhaps to throw in the towel, or alternatively to get back in the saddle.

Partners in Crime

HOLMES & WATSON

A Study in Scarlet, The Sign of Four, The Memoirs of Sherlock Holmes, The Adventures of Sherlock Holmes, The Return of Sherlock Holmes, The Hound of the Baskervilles, The Case Book of Sherlock Holmes by Arthur Conan Doyle

Consulting detective Sherlock Holmes and his friend Dr Watson solve singular crimes from their legendary bachelor apartment at 221B Baker Street.

ARTHUR CONAN DOYLE (1859–1930) fitted his writing around his work as a doctor for a number of years before deciding he would devote his time mainly to a literary career (although he also tried politics, ophthalmology and finally spiritualism). Holmes and Watson first appeared in *A Study in Scarlet* (first published in *Beeton's Christmas Annual*, 1887) and became well established after Doyle's second novel, *The Sign of Four*, was published in both the USA and the UK in 1894. His agent then negotiated a publishing deal for subsequent Holmes and Watson stories with *Strand* magazine. When Doyle – wishing to be taken seriously as an author of literary fiction – killed off his famous detective in 1893, the magazine lost thousands of subscribers. He restored Holmes to life in 1903, following a lucrative publishing deal.

According to Doyle's memoirs, SHERLOCK HOLMES is partially inspired by Dr Joseph Bell, who taught Doyle medicine at Edinburgh University and was renowned for his powers of deduction and diagnosis through logic and observation. Holmes famously wears an ear-flapped travelling cap, carries a magnifying glass and plays the violin. He has grey, deep-set eyes, a long nose, thin white fingers and gaunt limbs. Despite this physique, he is a champion boxer and swordsman. Addicted to stimulants, Holmes takes snuff, drinks coffee and injects cocaine. He also smokes strong tobacco, which he keeps in a Persian slipper. As a result, he alternates between 'excellent spirits' and 'fits of the blackest depression'.[11] Holmes is a master of disguises, is rather conceited and likes to make dramatic revelations. He has a 'cold, incisive, ironical voice', and a 'catlike love of personal cleanliness'.[12]

DR JOHN WATSON was formerly a medical officer in the British Army, attached to the Berkshires in the Second Afghan War. He was shot in the shoulder (and wounded in the leg), and then suffered a bout of dysentery, all of which ruined his health and brought him back to London. He is an ex-rugby player with a thick-set build; he smokes ship's tobacco and wears a moustache. Holmes describes him as a man of action, and he is not afraid to use his old service revolver. In the early stories Watson is still in convalescence and likes to lie in late in the Baker Street apartment. Nevertheless, he is stimulated by the promise of adventure. He marries Mary Morstan, one of Holmes's clients, and for a time has his own medical practice in Paddington. Watson takes detailed notes of Holmes's cases and is the narrator in almost all of the stories.

HOLMES ON WATSON

there is no man who is better worth having
at your side when you are in a tight place.

WATSON ON HOLMES

It was worth a wound – it was worth many
wounds – to know the depth of loyalty and
love which lay behind that cold mask.

HOLMES AND WATSON go together like bread and butter. Both characters are household names: they have taken on a life beyond the page in numerous adaptations over the course of the last century, and 'elementary, my dear Watson' is a catchphrase known the world over, even though Doyle never actually wrote those exact words (they first appear in a scriptwriter's adaptation).

Doyle's genius – perhaps inspired by Edgar Allan Poe's anonymous narrator of 'The Murders in the Rue Morgue', widely credited as the first detective story – lies in having Dr Watson narrate the details of each case. Through Watson we can see Holmes's extraordinary mind at work, with him we learn the 'science of deduction' and by his side we experience the emotional rollercoaster of each crime, while Holmes (like Poe's C. Auguste Dupin, whom Watson recalls in *A Study in Scarlet*) remains calm, collected and aloof (character traits which can clearly be seen in Agatha Christie's narrator Captain Hastings and his reverence for Hercule Poirot). Watson's admiration for Holmes is infectious, but it is not wholly unqualified, and we are likely to agree with him when he occasionally describes his friend as 'conceited' (Holmes dismisses Watson's comparison to Dupin, whom he regards as 'a very inferior fellow'[13] in a cheeky homage to Poe) and is annoyed by his 'bumptious' way of talking. 'One of Sherlock Holmes's defects – if indeed, one may call it a defect – was that he was exceedingly loath to communicate his full plans to another person until the instant of their fulfilment',[14] Watson complains, and of course this ramps up the dramatic tension for the reader. It is so much more compelling to have an eyewitness account of each case from an intimate friend than it would be to hear Holmes's own clinical, scientific and bloodless descriptions of his methodology.

Giving Holmes a companion (the two are first introduced by a mutual friend because Watson is looking for affordable rooms and Holmes needs someone to split the rent with him) also enables Doyle to make great use of dialogue throughout the stories. This quickens the pace, enables him to impart information in a colourful way, and further develops the characters of the investigating duo. Holmes himself remarks on it: 'nothing clears up a case so much as stating it to another person'.[15] It also helps to convey the irresistible sense of adventure that has made these stories appeal across generations. 'Now is the dramatic moment of fate, Watson, when you hear a step upon the stair which is walking into your life, and you know not whether for good or ill', says Holmes, with relish, at the start of *The Hound of the Baskervilles*. In a later story, when Watson has married and temporarily moved out of 221B, Holmes lures him back to a case with this tantalizing exchange:

'By the way, Doctor, I shall want your co-operation.'
  'I shall be delighted.'
  'You don't mind breaking the law?'
  'Not in the least.'
  'Nor running a chance of arrest?'
  'Not in a good cause.'
  'Oh, the cause is excellent!'
  'Then I am your man.'[16]

Watson's control of the narrative also helps to elevate him above the role of a mere sidekick. He learns from Holmes and applies Holmes's methodology. 'I have not lived for years with Sherlock Holmes for nothing' he says, after successfully manipulating Dr Mortimer in *The Hound of the Baskervilles*.[17] In that story, Holmes more or less delegates the case to Watson after being impressed by the series of deductions he has made from a walking cane which their new client has left behind:

> 'Really, Watson, you excel yourself,' said Holmes, pushing back his chair and lighting a cigarette. 'I am bound to say that in all the accounts which you have been so good as to give of my own small achievements you have habitually underrated your own abilities. It may be that you are not yourself luminous, but you are a conductor of light.'[18]

As Watson notes in 'A Scandal in Bohemia', lack of emotion is one of Holmes's key characteristics. Holmes has already declared that he will never marry, though Watson sees he is attracted to the masterly and beautiful performer Irene Adler, 'All emotions ... were abhorrent to his cold, precise but admirably balanced mind.'[19] But Watson himself seems to be an exception: Holmes is not without concern and warmth towards his friend. In their first adventure he empathizes with Watson's discomfort:

> 'What's the matter? You're not looking quite yourself. This Brixton Road affair has upset you.'
>
> 'To tell the truth, it has,' I said. 'I ought to be more case-hardened after my Afghan experiences. I saw my own comrades hacked to pieces at Maiwand without losing my nerve.'
>
> 'I can understand. There is a mystery about this which stimulates the imagination; where there is no imagination there is no horror.'[20]

He also seems genuinely to fear for his friend's safety as Watson sets out for Devon in *The Hound of the Baskervilles*:

> 'It's an ugly business, Watson, an ugly, dangerous business, and the more I see of it the less I like it. Yes, my dear fellow, you may laugh, but I give you my word that I shall be very glad to have you back safe and sound in Baker Street once more.'[21]

In the Ryder Street adventure, when Watson is actually shot in the leg, Holmes is uncharacteristically almost overcome with emotion: 'The clear, hard eyes were dimmed for a moment, and the firm lips were shaking. For the one and only time I caught a glimpse of a great heart as well as of a great brain.'[22]

For his part, Watson overcomes his tendency towards tact and reticence when he witnesses Holmes's addiction to cocaine, and speaks out of a sense of responsibility for Holmes's health:

> 'Why should you, for a mere passing pleasure, risk the loss of those great powers with which you have been endowed?

Remember that I speak not only as one comrade to another, but as a medical man to one for whose constitution he is to some extent answerable.'[23]

He has gained Holmes's trust enough, by 'The Adventure of the Missing Three-Quarter', to have 'weaned' him off the drug. But perhaps their most poignant moment comes when Holmes dramatically reappears at Watson's house, three years after his disappearance and supposed death at the hands of arch enemy Professor Moriarty, at the Reichenbach Falls in Switzerland. Watson faints at the surprise, and when he comes round he can't help gripping Holmes's arms to make sure he is real. Holmes tells him that after being undercover for so long, 'I found myself in my old armchair in my own old room, and only wishing that I could have seen my old friend Watson in the other chair which he has so often adorned.' Knowing that Watson's wife has recently died, he offers comfort in the only way he can:

'Work is the best antidote to sorrow, my dear Watson,' said he; 'and I have a piece of work for us both to-night which, if we can bring it to a successful conclusion, will in itself justify a man's life on this planet.[24]

The eager magazine subscribers must have raised a cheer as they read Watson's vivid description of the start of another ripping case: 'It was indeed like old times when, at that hour, I found myself seated beside him in a hansom, my revolver in my pocket, and the thrill of adventure in my heart.'[25] Soon, Watson has sold his practice and taken up residence once more at 221B Baker Street. Thus the brilliant partnership whose influence can be traced in many other detective duos – from Hercule Poirot and Captain Hastings to maverick Inspector Morse and Sergeant Lewis, and more recently Inspector John Rebus and Constable Siobhan Clarke – is resumed for many further adventures.

Host and Guest

RATTY *&* MOLE

The Wind in the Willows by Kenneth Grahame

Mole abandons his spring cleaning in search of adventure. Reaching the river bank, he soon befriends Ratty, Otter and Badger and together they form a plan to rescue and reform the overexcitable Toad of Toad Hall and to liberate his home from the Wild Wooders.

The characters in *The Wind in the Willows* first appeared in bedtime stories told by KENNETH GRAHAME (1859–1932) to his only child, Alastair, and continued in letters (now preserved in the Bodleian Library) sent home while the Grahame parents holidayed in Cornwall. Published in 1908, the book initially received mixed reviews in the UK but became a great success in the USA, following an endorsement by President Roosevelt. It was adapted for the stage by A.A. Milne (see p. 32) in 1929 and has since become a classic of children's literature.

MOLE wears a black velvet smoking jacket and sometimes a cap and a pair of galoshes. He is impatient – first with spring cleaning, then with learning how to row, and later with wanting to meet Badger in the Wild Wood. But this is because he revels in new experiences and he wants to learn how to get on in riverbank society. Mole's unquenchable enthusiasm sometimes bursts out endearingly and he often exclaims 'O my! O my!' He heartily appreciates a well-laid supper table and luxurious comforts provided to him first by Ratty and then at Badger's house.

RATTY has a round face, whiskers, twinkly eyes, 'small neat ears' and 'thick silky hair'. He loves the river and 'messing about in boats', together with daydreaming and writing poetry. He can hear words and songs in the whispering of the wind through the reeds of the riverbank. Of independent means, Ratty delights in providing hospitality to his friends and is optimistic in a crisis. Critics have speculated that he is modelled on the scholar and experienced boatman F.J. Furnivall, a close friend of Grahame's, or possibly Grahame's brother Roland, whose nickname was Ratty.

MOLE ON RATTY

You ought to go where you'll be properly appreciated. You're simply wasted here, among us fellows. If only I had your head, Ratty.

RATTY ON MOLE

I feel just as you do, Mole... It's lucky we've got the stream with us, to take us home. Isn't it jolly to feel the sun again, soaking into one's bones. And hark to the wind playing in the reeds.

ONE OF THE most appealing features of *The Wind in the Willows* is its concern with home comforts: buttered toast, bacon and eggs, roaring fires; a picnic hamper filled with cold chicken, sandwiches, French rolls and pickled gherkins; mulled ale on a cold winter's night; lemonade on a sunny day. All of these are made even more enjoyable when provided by a good-natured host and enthusiastically accepted by an appreciative guest.

Ratty's easy hospitality towards Mole, who appears out of the blue one spring day on the riverbank opposite his home, sets the tone for the reciprocal nature of their friendship – Ratty's generosity is matched by Mole's intoxication with his new experience:

> 'Look here! If you've really nothing else on hand this morn-
> ing, supposing we drop down the river together, and have a
> long day of it?'
> The Mole waggled his toes from sheer happiness, spread
> his chest with a sigh of contentment, and leaned back
> blissfully into the soft cushions. '*What* a day I'm having!' he
> said. 'Let us start at once!'[26]

Ratty is the perfect host, providing not only a picnic (and a beautiful picnic spot) but later dressing gown and slippers, supper and a comfortable pillow in the best bedroom, which has the river lapping outside its window. He is keen for Mole to understand his affection for the river: 'It's brother and sister to me, and aunts, and company, and food and drink... It's my world, and I don't want any other',[27] and he promises to teach him how to swim and row and introduces him to his friends along the riverbank.

Ratty's love for his riverside home spills over into poetry and wanting others to share it, but also sits deep within him and causes homesickness. This creates a tension between the love of home and the desire for new experiences which runs through the story, embodied by the two animals. On first meeting Toad, Mole is thrilled by the idea of going on an adventure in his new caravan. Ratty is not at all keen, but, being the perfect host, he goes along with it because 'he hated disappointing people, and he was fond of Mole, and would do almost anything to oblige him'. Once on the road, though, he is afflicted by a strong desire for home, and Mole, for all his delight in the 'canary-coloured cart and all its little fitments', instinctively understands:

> 'I *don't* talk about my river... But I *think* about it... I think about it – all the time!'
> The Mole reached out from under his blanket, felt for the Rat's paw in the darkness, and gave it a squeeze. 'I'll do whatever you like, Ratty,' he whispered. 'Shall we run away tomorrow morning ... and go back to our dear old hole on the river?'[28]

Later, when Mole is himself suddenly struck by home-sickness, like an 'electric shock' on the way back through the Wild Wood, he too is torn between accompanying his friend to the river or following his nose back to his own home,

> But even under such a test as this his loyalty to his friend stood firm. Never for a moment did he dream of abandoning him. Meanwhile the wafts from his old home pleaded, whispered, conjured, and finally claimed him imperiously.[29]

Ratty understands and bravely returns with him through the cold darkness: 'I tell you, I'm going to find this place now, if I stay out all night. So cheer up, old chap, and take my arm, and we'll very soon be back there again.' Once at Mole End, he kindly ignores the dust and encourages Mole to give him a tour of the house in order to make his friend feel better: 'No wonder you're so fond of it, Mole. Tell us all about it, and how you came to make it what it is.'[30] Though initially dismayed that there is 'not a crumb' he can offer his friend, Mole's own modest hospitality is acknowledged when the carol-singing field mice come knocking, confident that as in previous years they will get hot drinks and supper from the last residence on their round.

But while Mole's love of 'a place which was all his own' gives him the anchor he needs to enable him to venture further afield to the riverbank and even the Wild Wood, Ratty's connection to the river makes him extremely uncomfortable, even ill, whenever he faces the prospect of leaving it. He doesn't even want to think about what lies further than he can see: 'Beyond the Wild Wood comes the Wide World', he tells Mole. 'And that's something that doesn't matter, either to you or me.'[31] Though he does bravely rescue Mole after he impatiently goes off on an adventure of his own to find Badger's house and becomes lost and terrified in the wood, it is Ratty who is most keen to return to his 'faithful, steady-going old river'[32] as soon as possible.

Like Mole, who answers the call of spring and comes up for air, Ratty too is affected by the seasons, and he grows restless as the swallows prepare for migration at the end of the summer. After hearing the adventures of a seafaring rat in Greece, Italy and Turkey, he decides he must head south too, but Mole sees that his friend is in a kind of trance, mechanically packing a satchel while his mind is disengaged. So it is that Mole, the adventurer, stops Ratty from leaving and waits for the 'strange seizure to pass'.[33] Knowing his friend well by now, as he recovers, he brings him pencil and paper, in the hope that his hobby of writing poetry will lift his spirits. It is the equivalent of the talking therapy Ratty provides at Mole End.

Both animals are key to the eventual reclamation of Toad Hall from the Wild Wooders, who are not so much unwelcome guests as aggressive occupiers, and are trashing the place in Toad's absence. Mole enters into the operation with more enthusiasm than Ratty and even adopts Toad's washerwoman disguise to goad the stoats guarding the gates. Ratty, anxious at what they will face there, and ever the considerate host, provides them all with pistols, swords, truncheons, flasks and sandwiches.

Their success is celebrated with formal hospitality in the form of a banquet for friends and neighbours, given by Toad but organized and closely managed by Badger because 'it is expected … – in fact it's the rule'. But under Badger's strict orders, Toad is somewhat depressed, and the event is not very enjoyable. Toad's hospitality is inadequate without prompting from Badger and he still has to learn how to be a responsible member of the privileged class, as Badger knows well: 'This good fellow has got to live here, and hold his own, and be respected.'

More fun is had by Ratty and Mole the day after their victory, when they sit in comfortable wicker chairs in Toad's garden, 'roaring with laughter and kicking their short legs up in the air'. Perhaps Grahame is using them as models of behaviour, in an attempt to demonstrate how the status quo of class privilege might be maintained through social responsibility, against a growing movement for social change (in 1908 the women's suffrage movement was gaining momentum and the Labour Party was also garnering support).[34] Or perhaps he was subconsciously sending a message to his young son that he was better off staying at home, even though his parents had gone on holiday without him. Whatever the message, Mole's and Ratty's easy hospitality towards everyone enables them both to live the rest of their lives, whether by the river or underground, or in the Wild Wood, in appreciation and respect for their surroundings, and in 'great joy and contentment'.[35]

Heroes of Middle-earth

FRODO & SAM

The Lord of the Rings by J.R.R. Tolkien

Frodo Baggins comes into possession of 'one Ring to rule them all' and must destroy it in the heart of deadly Mordor in order to save his own home of the Shire, the lands of Men and all Middle-earth. He is accompanied on his quest by Samwise Gamgee, Merry Brandybuck, Pippin Took, Gandalf the Wizard, Legolas the Elf, Gimli the Dwarf, and Strider and Boromir (both Men).

J.R.R. TOLKIEN (1892–1973) wrote *The Lord of the Rings* between 1937 and 1949, partly during the Second World War; it was published in three volumes in 1954–5 and went on to become a monumental bestseller. But it is the First World War, in which all but one of Tolkien's close friends were killed, which seems to have informed his writing, specifically the relationship between Sam and Frodo within the tale. In a letter written to H. Cotton Minchin Tolkien explained that the character of Samwise was inspired by the privates and batmen he knew during the war, combined with memories of village children.[36] Tolkien designed dust jackets for all three volumes; these, along with many of his original drawings and maps of Middle-earth, are among the Tolkien papers in the Bodleian Library.

FRODO BAGGINS is taller and fairer than the other hobbits in the Shire. He has bright eyes and a cleft chin, and he is shy, eccentric and gentle. Orphaned by the drowning of both his parents, Frodo has been adopted by Bilbo and, at the start of the tale, lives with him at Bag End. Frodo's birthday is 22 September; by the age of fifty he is restless, and misses Bilbo, who secretly left to join the Elves at Rivendell on his iiith birthday. He is afraid of dogs. He tells Gandalf: 'I feel very small, and very uprooted, and well – desperate.'[37] But Gandalf, who knows the Baggins family well, comments: 'You take after Bilbo. ... There is more about you than meets the eye.'[38]

SAMWISE GAMGEE is Frodo's rather rotund gardener. He lives at 3 Bagshot Row with his father, who is known as the Gaffer. He is prone to blushing and sudden fits of tears, but Frodo describes him as 'stout-hearted' and he is often compared to a faithful dog. Sam's sharp hearing and ability to eavesdrop often get Frodo out of trouble. Though he loves the Shire, he also adores stories about the old days. Sam likes beer (he says a special goodbye to the barrel at Bag End before departure) and is a good cook and an excellent quartermaster. He carries saucepans and a portable stove for most of their journey. 'Gamgee' is a now obsolete word for cotton wool, but it is also a surname: in 1956 a real-life Sam Gamgee from Essex wrote to Tolkien asking how he had come across the name.[39]

F RIENDS of all shapes and sizes help Frodo on his quest to release Middle-earth from the evil power of Sauron. The nine selected at the Council of Elrond form a special, lifelong bond. But of all these, it is Samwise Gamgee, with Frodo from the first to the last, who demonstrates to him and to us the power of deep friendship in the face of paralysing horror, a horror that encompasses the faceless dark riders, giant Orcs and Trolls, an enormous venomous spider and the fiery perils of Mount Doom itself.

As befits a quest narrative, the two hobbits are unlikely heroes, and Frodo is at first reluctant to take on the burden of the Ring he has inherited from Bilbo. 'I am not made for perilous quests. I wish I had never seen the Ring!'[40] he tells Gandalf, once he has learnt how dangerous its power is. But Sam, eavesdropping below the window as he pretends to trim the grass, couldn't be more excited at the prospect of setting out. Once Gandalf has caught him and made him confess what he has heard, the wizard impetuously punishes him by commanding him to accompany Frodo, and Sam's reaction is rather different:

> 'Me, sir!' cried Sam, springing up like a dog invited for a walk. 'Me go and see Elves and all! Hooray!' he shouted, and then burst into tears.[41]

Both Frodo's seriousness and Sam's enthusiasm for stories about the Elves will help them through the times ahead. And there's nothing like a loyal and amusing friend to encourage the reader's emotional investment in the hero's struggles (something Dickens used to good effect in *Great Expectations*, see p. 67).

If Sam, as Tolkien wrote in his letter to H. Cotton Minchin, is similar to an English soldier, then Frodo perhaps has some similarities with an inexperienced officer put in charge of a dangerous mission. Frodo has an acute sense of responsibility for his friends and the peril he is taking them towards. Even before they have left the Shire, Frodo decides it would be better for him to go on alone:

> 'It is one thing to take my young friends walking over the Shire with me, until we are hungry and weary, and food and bed are sweet. To take them into exile, where hunger and weariness may have no cure, is quite another. ... I don't think I ought even to take Sam.'[42]

Again, after Boromir's treachery on Amon Hen, Frodo can no longer bear the thought of losing his friends and he uses the invisibility powers of the Ring to give them the slip. Sam, though, anticipates him, and intercepts his boat, refusing to let him go alone, and they have this exchange:

> 'I couldn't have a borne it, it'd have been the death of me.'
>   'It would be the death of you to come with me, Sam,' said Frodo, 'and I could not have borne that.'
>   'Not as certain as being left behind,' said Sam.
>   'But I am going to Mordor.'
>   'I know that well enough, Mr. Frodo. Of course you are. And I'm coming with you.'[43]

Frodo's sense of responsibility for his friends is mirrored by Sam's sense of responsibility for Frodo, and Sam's single-minded focus on keeping Frodo fed, watered and rested means that Frodo can put all his energies into the task given to him: the responsibility of destroying the Ring before the enemy can take it. Sam cooks for Frodo, packs for him, keeps watch over him while he sleeps (even if this means he has to press his own knuckles into his eyes to keep awake), and gives him his own share of food and water. Their intertwined fate is symbolized by their last tremendous effort, overcoming exhaustion to reach the fiery depths of Mount Doom, when Sam says:

> 'I can't carry it for you, but I can carry you and it as well. So up you get! … Sam will give you a ride. Just tell him where to go, and he'll go.'[44]

When the eagles rescue them after the Ring has been destroyed, they find the two friends hand in hand, awaiting death.

While battles rage around them – armies of Men often under inadequate leaders trying to hold off the immense battalions of Orcs raised by Saruman and Sauron – the Hobbits rely on instinct, not firepower, to get them through, and they learn to trust it. When Boromir argues that they should join the wars of Gondor, Frodo tells him 'it would seem like wisdom but for the warning of my heart'.[45] Sam holds back from attacking Gollum, even when it becomes clear that Gollum is intending to kill him, because 'deep in his heart there was something that restrained him'[46] (a wise decision, since it is Gollum, in the end, who destroys the Ring). And, realizing that after Shelob's attack Frodo is not dead but unconscious, he chastises himself for overthinking:

> 'You fool … your heart knew it. Don't trust your head, Samwise, it is not the best part of you.'[47]

The Hobbits' trust in their hearts is linked also to an acceptance of fate. Sam's mistakes can sometimes find them a route out of trouble – as when he gets drawn in by Faramir's tales of the Elves and lets slip that Frodo has the Ring: 'be comforted, Samwise', Faramir (Boromir's younger brother) says. 'If you seem to have stumbled, think that it was fated to be so. Your heart is shrewd as well as faithful, and saw clearer than your eyes ... it was safe to declare this to me. It may even help the master that you love.'[48] And, indeed, they are given protection and provisions by Faramir at the Window of the Sunset and sent on their way.

Frodo's and Sam's sense of fate is also inextricably bound up with the feeling that they are part of an ongoing story, one of the stories Sam so loved to hear from Bilbo back in the Shire. On the Stairs of Cririth Ungol, when they have eaten what Frodo thinks may be their last meal, they talk about the old tales. Sam says he used to think folk went looking for adventure, but now he realizes that no protagonist knows how their story will end. He goes on to imagine their story written down in a 'great big book with red and black letters', and Frodo, in an echo of Sancho's pride at becoming a literary character (see p. 131), is immensely cheered by this idea:

'Why Sam,' he said, 'to hear you somehow makes me as merry as if the story was already written. But you've left out one of the chief characters: Samwise the stouthearted. "I want to hear more about Sam, dad. Why didn't they put in more of his talk, dad? That's what I like, it makes me laugh. And Frodo wouldn't have got far without Sam, would he, dad?"'[49]

At the end of *The Return of the King*, when Sam is happily married to Rosie Cotton, and Frodo has decided to leave the Shire forever and join Bilbo in the undying lands, Frodo comforts his best friend with the thought that their story will endure: 'You will read things out of the Red Book and keep alive the memory of the age that is gone.'[50]

And so Sam returns to the idyllic setting of the Shire, proving Gandalf's instinct both at Bag End and the Council of Elrond ('it would be well to trust rather to their friendship than great wisdom'[51]) to be spot on. The success of the quest depended primarily, in the end, not on battles, brains or brinkmanship, but on two friends bound together by love and responsibility.

Hard Times

A DUTY TO BEAR WITNESS is felt by many of the friends featured in narratives of times of hardship, be it a future dystopia, a period of extreme social inequality or a colonial invasion. Offred does her best to tell and preserve her best friend Moira's story even though she does not know how it ends; despite their differences, Obierika has the courage to explain his friend Okonkwo's towering reputation to the ignorant white missionaries; John Steinbeck's novella is in part an attempt to explain an incident he saw in real life. In recent years, Elena Ferrante's four-book series examines almost every conceivable angle of a friendship formed in childhood in an impoverished district of Naples and developed through adult life, setting the bar very high indeed for future writers wishing to explore our need for friends and our enduring desire to record and reinterpret friendships over the course of a lifetime.

Loneliest in the World

GEORGE & LENNIE

Of Mice and Men by John Steinbeck

George and Lennie are itinerant farmworkers, moving
from ranch to ranch across California during the Great
Depression. When they join a ranch near Soledad, they find
themselves singled out for abuse by the ranch-owner's son,
Curley. George does his best to protect Lennie, but tragically
he can't keep his friend out of trouble for long.

JOHN STEINBECK (1902–1968) developed the idea for *Of Mice and
Men* from his own experience of working on the ranches of his
native California in the 1920s under racial segregation and during
the economic depression. In an interview with the *New York Times* he
described witnessing an incident in which a farmhand killed a ranch
foreman and was put into an asylum. Originally, the book was called
'Something That Happened', a deliberately neutral title to indicate
the absence of authorial opinion in the novella.[1] 'Of Mice and Men'
is a quotation from 'To a Mouse' by Robert Burns ('The best laid
schemes o' Mice an' Men / Gang aft agley'). Steinbeck envisaged the
text as a novel that could be performed, not least because large parts
of it are in dialogue. Published in 1937, it soon hit the bestseller lists

and was also adapted into a successful play. But it is still controversial, and is frequently banned by school boards in the USA.

GEORGE MILTON is small and lithe, he has a swarthy complexion and red-rimmed eyes from the sun: 'Every part of him was defined: small, strong hands, slender arms, a thin and bony nose.'[2] He grew up in Auburn but no longer has any close family. The other farmworkers think he is smart, and he is good at cards. His personal possessions amount to a bedroll, a razor, a bar of soap, a comb, a bottle of pills and liniment. Like Lennie, he wears a denim jacket, denim trousers and a black hat.

LENNIE SMALL is described early on in complete contrast to George: 'a huge man, shapeless of face, with large, pale eyes, with wide, sloping shoulders'.[3] He is often compared to animals: he walks like a bear, he is strong as a bull, or loyal as a terrier. He has been brought up by his Aunt Clara in Auburn and since her death has been looked after by George. Lennie has learning disabilities and is enormously strong but gentle in disposition. Slim says he is just like a child. He likes to touch things that feel soft and he loves to pet animals: mice, puppies, rabbits. Overall, he is happier than George.

THE NATURALISTIC DIALOGUE between friends Lennie and George makes up large parts of this novella. As the plot unfolds, we realize that their colourful conversations are full of repeated motifs and stories. They are so familiar with each other's speech and ideas that they can finish sentences for each other, indicating a long and intimate companionship. So, at the start of the novel, when they are resting by a pool on their way to another ranch, George's exasperation with Lennie – 'God, you're a lot of trouble... I could get along so easy and so nice if I didn't have you on my tail. I would live so easy and maybe have a girl'[4] – is something Lennie has heard many times before. To hear it again is comforting because it is so familiar. He knows that eventually George will feel ashamed of his outburst, and then he will be able to entice him to talk about how they are different from the other ranch workers – 'the loneliest guys in the world'[5] – because they have each other, and this will lead on to talking about their dream of buying a small farm of their own, with rabbits for him to look after, which is what he loves to hear about most of all. Their conversations follow variations of this pattern several times in the book.

We learn more about the nature of George and Lennie's friendship after they arrive at the ranch near Soledad and George opens up to the sympathetic mule-driver, Slim. Slim is intrigued by it, since most of the farmworkers operate in isolation:

'I hardly never seen two guys travel together. You know how the hands are, they just come in and get their bunk and work a month, and then they quit and go out alone. Never seem to give a damn about nobody.'[6]

George explains that at first he used to play tricks on Lennie and get him to do foolish things, until one day he told him to jump in a river and he nearly drowned. Then he grew to appreciate Lennie's extraordinary strength and stamina, which must have helped them to get work at a time when any job was hard to come by. 'We kinda look after each other', George explains, 'I've knew him for a long time.'[7] The value and rarity of their friendship are underscored by responses from both

Candy (the old man who cleans the bunkhouses) and Crooks (a stable-hand, cruelly not allowed in the bunkhouses under segregation because he is black), who quickly overcome their initial suspicions to ask if they too can join in the plan to buy a small farm and live off the fat of the land. George loves to talk about this as much as Lennie loves to listen to it. It transports them from the grim reality of their back-breaking, low-paid work and their squalid bunkhouse, and others quickly see it as a remedy for loneliness and isolation.

Having quickly appraised the other workers, George warns Lennie to stay away from Curley's wife, anticipating a dangerous situation which Lennie wouldn't be able to understand. He tries to teach him to be gentle with the puppy Slim has given to him. He tries to speak up for him and convey how proud he is of Lennie's strength, stamina and obedience. George's loneliness is offset by having someone to look after, however difficult that becomes. Even when the body of Curley's wife is discovered, and it is clear to everyone that Lennie has (unintentionally) broken her neck, he defends his friend:

> 'Lennie never done it in meanness,' he said. 'All the time he done bad things, but he never done one of 'em mean.'[8]

A parallel episode involving Candy's old, blind, lame dog partially prepares us for the horrific conclusion of the novella. Candy can't bear to put the dog down because he's been such a good working sheepdog over the years. But he puts up no real resistance when Carlson – a tough ranch-hand – takes the dog outside to shoot it. Candy later admits to George that he should have killed the dog himself instead of letting a stranger do it.

Lennie himself has a moment of lucidity as he waits for George by the pool of the Salinas river, under the ridge of the Gabilan mountains, where we found the two friends at the start of the story. His Aunt Clara appears to him in a kind of dream and recalls all George's past kindnesses: 'He been doin' nice things for you alla time. When he got a piece a pie you always got half or more'n half. An' if they was any ketchup, why he'd give it all to you.' Lennie calls out for his friend, and when George appears he begs him: 'You ain't gonna leave me, are ya, George? I know you ain't.'[9]

Slim and George both understand the fate awaiting Lennie: he'll either be shot by Curley or strapped down by the police and put in a cage. George promises Lennie he won't leave him and believes in that moment that for Lennie to be alone for the rest of his life would be worse than dying. As Curley and the other men from the ranch draw closer, George's ultimate act of friendship is to give Lennie the most compassionate death he can manage – a single shot to the back of the head (with Carlson's gun) – even as they rehearse the well-worn lines of the conversation which started the story, and Lennie pictures the farm, with the rabbits he has long dreamed of looking after.

Should we condemn George for his act of euthanasia? For denying Lennie a proper trial, even one that would be likely to end with him facing the death penalty (execution by hanging at that time). Or does this show how fragile friendship is in the face of extreme deprivation? There is no authorial voice guiding us. But throughout the portrayal of this unusual friendship we have seen compassion win out in George's internal struggle between exasperation and pity. In the most inhumane situations, any kind of companionship is better than none – something Crooks has articulated in his own encounter with Lennie. 'Poor bastard', George whispers after one of his own enraged outbursts.[10] 'Poor bastard', Candy says, while sitting with the dead body of Curley's wife.[11] None of the labourers who follow George criticize him for what he's done, and there is no authorial comment. At the end of the book, it is Slim who offers a small glimmer of hope to George, sitting down close beside him and telling him: 'A guy got to sometimes.' The possibility of a new friendship is tentatively hinted at, as he helps grieving George to his feet and takes him off for a drink to drown his sorrows.

Kinship

OBIERIKA *&* OKONKWO

Things Fall Apart by Chinua Achebe

The novel narrates the life story of Okonkwo, a powerful clansman from Umuofia, a group of nine Igbo villages in Nigeria, at the start of the twentieth century. The first part chronicles his rise to power within the rules and culture of the clan. The second part describes his temporary exile for the accidental killing of a fellow clansman. The final part narrates tragic and violent events following the arrival of the white missionaries.

CHINUA ACHEBE (1930–2013) grew up in Ogidi in Eastern Nigeria. His father had joined the missionaries as a young man and Achebe was brought up as a Christian. But his great uncle, a powerful clan leader, lived nearby, and Achebe was also able to spend time with him and the tribe from which he was descended. Achebe took a degree at University College, Ibadan. He wrote *Things Fall Apart*, his first novel (and the first book in what would become *The African Trilogy*) at the age of twenty-seven, while working for the Nigerian Broadcasting Service. Though written in English and taking its title from 'The Second Coming' by W.B. Yeats, it was the first mainstream novel to tell a story from the perspective of the indigenous African population rather than a Western colonizer and had a lasting influence on literature about Africa. Published in 1958, two years before Nigeria's declaration of independence from British rule, it has since sold over 20 million copies.

OKONKWO is famous throughout the nine villages of Umuofia for having defeated a champion wrestler in a spectacular fight at the age of just nineteen. He is tall and well built, and walks as if he is about to pounce. His fearsome demeanour has earned him the nickname 'roaring flame'. Okonkwo has also proved himself a fierce warrior, having collected five human heads from two battles. His drive comes from a strong desire to be different from his father, who was lazy and accumulated debts. He has a slight stutter and finds it easier to communicate with his fists than through words (he is 'not a man of thought but of action').[12] His uncontrollable temper causes him to break not only the clan laws but also, later, the law imposed by the British.

OBIERIKA is Okonkwo's greatest friend. He is popular among the clansmen and also brave. His son, Maduka, is much admired by Okonkwo for his wrestling skills, and he is clearly respected by his daughter's suitor's family, who bring no fewer than fifty jars of palm wine to the marriage ceremony. He is wealthy enough in turn to make them a gift of a large goat. Like Okonkwo, he has risen through the clan to take the ozo title, reserved for only a select few. But Obierika is not afraid to debate the merits of clan law; he is a man 'who thought about things'[13] and does not act on impulse.

> *Things fall apart; the centre cannot hold;*
> *Mere anarchy is loosed upon the world*

T HINGS FALL APART is a groundbreaking and complex novel, driven by the brave, successful and uncompromising character of its main protagonist, Okonkwo. Like many tragic heroes before him, he is facing a seismic change to his way of life and he pits the full force of his flawed personality against it. Next to him at these moments of crisis is his best friend Obierika: critical, supportive, sympathetic and wise.

Obierika is first introduced into the story when Okonkwo is experiencing a very rare moment of self-doubt. The clan elders have decreed that Ikemefuna, a young boy given to Okonkwo by a rival village to atone for a murder and brought up by him as his favourite son, should be taken out of the village and killed. Okonkwo is not expected to participate in this act, but he chooses to accompany the elders because he hates to appear weak. When Ikemefuna is attacked and cries out for help from his stepfather, in a split-second Okonkwo sides with the tribe and kills him with his matchet. Ever since, he has had trouble sleeping and eating. He tries spending time with his biological son, Nwoye (who is afraid of him), drinking palm wine and taking snuff, but when these don't work he goes to see his great friend Obierika.

The two men know each other's children well, so that Okonkwo can compliment Maduka on his wrestling and Obierika can reassure Okonkwo that his own children are too young yet to be judged on their strength. Okonkwo is so focused on promoting his own sense of bravery that he turns his uneasiness at killing Ikemefuna into an interrogation of his friend: 'I cannot understand why you refused to come with us to kill that boy', he says, implying that Obierika is defying the village Oracle. Obierika's reply immediately demonstrates the difference between them. He has understood the Oracle, but since it did not specifically say that he should carry out the killing he chose not to go. He is able to think about and interpret the message before springing into action: 'if the Oracle said that my son should be killed I would neither dispute it nor be the one to do it',[14] he tells his friend, demonstrating a more philosophical approach.

Despite this difference in interpretation, the two friends offer each other practical support. Okonkwo helps Obierika to negotiate the bride price for his daughter, and Obierika looks out for Okonkwo when he has been exiled for seven years (for accidentally killing a fellow tribesman) by selling his yams for him and giving him the resulting bags of cowrie shells. Although Okonkwo accepts the rule of exile, he is deeply depressed by it. Obierika also complies with the clan's laws and helps to destroy Okonkwo's 'impure' compound, but when he has finished he questions his friend's misfortune: 'Why should a man suffer so grievously for an offence he had committed inadvertently? But although he thought for a long time he found no answer. He was merely led into greater complexities.'[15]

Obierika refers once more to his disagreement with Okonkwo over the death of Ikemefuna when Okonkwo ceremoniously asks him how he can repay the debt of gratitude for his help while in exile. 'Kill one of your sons for me', he says, harking back with morbid humour to the day Okonkwo murdered his adopted son. When his friend protests, Obierika exaggerates even further – 'Then kill yourself' – and in doing so fore-shadows events to come.

Obierika visits Okonkwo several times during his exile: first to bring him cowrie shells and then to comfort him when he learns that Nwoye has joined the missionaries. When his friend returns to the village, since Obierika is a man 'who thinks about things' he tries to interpret the ensuing events, while all Okonkwo can do is express dismay that no one is attacking the newcomers: 'What is it that has happened to our people? Why have they lost the power to fight?'[16] Obierika understands and tries to explain to his friend that their world has already been changed by the arrival of the white man: 'he has put a knife on the things that held us together and we have fallen apart.'[17] The British have guns, they have already wiped out the village of Abame, they have their own laws, prisons, schools and religion, and no regard for or understanding of the Igbo culture. They have convinced significant numbers from Umuofia to work for them. Warrior-style resistance, which is the only kind Okonkwo can contemplate, is now redundant.

Despite his friend's attempts to explain how different things are now, Okonkwo returns to Umuofia expecting attention and respect for his beautiful daughters of marriageable age and his son's readiness to take the uzo title, and is disappointed that the village focuses instead on the activities of the British missionaries and the district commissioner: he has underestimated the rate of change. Again, it is Obierika who describes to him the white man's far-reaching powers. They discuss a fight over some land in which Aneto has killed fellow clansman Oduce.

Aneto was ready to go into exile for killing Oduce according to the law of the clan. But the white men arrested him, and he was hanged according to British law. The two friends don't need to review or compare the systems of justice: the story says it all. Instead, they sit in silence together for a long time.

When Okonkwo and five other clan leaders are thrown in jail and beaten on the order of the commissioner for attacking the church, diplomatic Obierika attends a secret meeting and the village pays a fine for their release. But soon after, everyone in the village is summoned to a gathering at the marketplace to decide how to respond to the commissioner's actions. When Okonkwo calls for Obierika, who has looked after him on his return from jail, on his way to the meeting, Obierika is greeted by many friends en route. It is significant that Okonkwo has no interest in these interactions, unable to see that his actions have consequences for the entire community. When the meeting is interrupted by five British court messengers, Okonkwo is once again caught in a moment in which he feels he must prove his strength and leadership to the tribe, even though he now knows that what once held the tribe together has gone:

> the world seemed to stand still, waiting. There was utter silence. The men of Umuofia were merged into the mute backcloth of trees and giant creepers, waiting.[18]

Okonkwo kills the first messenger with his matchet. But the tribe does not follow his lead, and lets the others escape. Knowing what fate awaits him, Okonkwo later hangs himself.

Literary critics have described Okonkwo as a tragic hero, and there are some similarities between Okonkwo and Obierika's friendship and Hamlet and Horatio's (see p. 56). Both sets of friends are dealing with a rapidly changing world and both Horatio and Obierika look on with empathy but not with influence as the respective heroes grapple with a period of exile and the fatal consequences of their actions. Like Horatio at the end of *Hamlet*, Obierika is the survivor who must liaise with the incoming ruler. He patiently explains that the British must cut down Okonkwo's body since it is taboo for the clansmen to touch or bury the body of a suicide. He cannot fight the British officials, but he is brave enough to confront them with words:

'that man was one of the greatest men in Umuofia. You drove him to kill himself; and now he will be buried like a dog...'[19]

No matter how doubtful he is about some aspects of clan law, Obierika cannot bear to see an acclaimed warrior and friend dismissed with such ignorance by the British. We have already learned from the narrator that the sad story of Ikemefuna continues to be told; in the second book of the trilogy, *No Longer at Ease*, both Okonkwo and Obierika are remembered as being 'great in their day', their bond surviving both the internal and the external conflicts faced by their clan.

Amazon Sisters

CELIE, SHUG & SOFIA

The Color Purple by Alice Walker

Set in rural Georgia in the 1930s, the novel is narrated by
Celie, a fourteen-year-old African-American girl born into a
poor family. She has been raped by her stepfather (who she
thinks is her biological father), given birth to a girl and a
boy who have both been taken away, her mother has recently
died, she is married to an abusive man who is in love with
somebody else, and her sister Nettie has left home. Through
encounters with two strong but contrasting women, singer
Shug Avery and daughter-in-law Sofia Butler, Celie learns
how to survive her abuse and find an independent role for
herself.

Published in 1982, *The Color Purple* won the Pulitzer Prize for Fiction
and has since sold over 5 million copies. It was made into a successful
film in 1985. ALICE WALKER grew up in Georgia during segregation;
her parents were sharecroppers and her mother also worked as a
seamstress. She has talked about witnessing the violence of her
grandfather towards her grandmother and wanting to tell a story
for and about her ancestors, for which she (like Mark Twain before

her; see p. 15) carefully chose a vernacular voice. Although some have criticized the novel for its depiction of black male violence, and it is frequently banned in schools, there is no doubt that it has become a landmark of African-American literature in the twentieth century.

MISS CELIE has learnt at a young age that survival in her community means being obedient and keeping quiet. Several characters in the book describe Celie as 'ugly' and 'shape funny' and she complains of her own 'nappy' hair. Although she is skinny, she is strong and can do the same work as a man in the cotton field. Her other skills include sewing, cooking and nursing. She particularly likes to cut and dress hair. As a young child she loved school. Her belief in God is strong until shaken by her discovery of her husband's deception. The main part of the narrative is told in her uneducated voice, but through this her sense of humour and powers of observation shine.

SOFIA BUTLER is smart and pretty with bright skin. She is also big and strong – 'Solid, like if she sit down on something, it be mash'[20] – and determined to do what she wants without compromise. When she is angry – which is often – her ears move up and down. She fights like a man and drives like a maniac. She also takes on hard work, fixing the roof of her house and building a swing in the garden. Although her punishment is completely out of proportion to her offence, once she is free from prison and slavery she swiftly moves on with her life and even maintains a close relationship with the white girl whose maid she was forced to be.

SHUG AVERY, 'Queen Honeybee', is a beautiful and glamorous singer from Memphis who has left her three children behind with her parents to pursue her career in showbusiness. Preachers describe her as a slut, hussy, strumpet and tramp. She is skinny as a bean, often wears red, and when Celie first sees her in person 'it like the trees all round the house draw themself up tall for a better look'.[21] Shug's life is on the road; she has seen far more of the world than any of the other characters and it has not been easy.

IT'S HARD TO THINK of a fictional character more in need of a friend than Miss Celie. Having been ordered by her rapist stepfather to tell 'nobody but God',[22] she takes him literally and narrates her story in letters to the Almighty. Isolated by the abuse she has suffered, she has no one to talk to, no one to confide in. It is only Celie's belief in heaven and her love for her younger sister Nettie that give her an inner resilience despite the appalling treatment she endures. And, early on in the novel, the sight of a glamorous photo of singer Shug Avery and an encounter with her stepson's feisty girlfriend, Sofia, give her something beyond everyday life to dream about and a courageous example to follow.

But like so many friends in fiction, at their first meeting, when Celie's husband Albert (Mr —) brings Shug home to recuperate from a serious illness, she seems more like an enemy. 'You sure is ugly', Shug says, scrutinizing Celie with mean eyes. Celie thinks this meanness is what will keep her alive – 'she weak as a kitten. But her mouth just pack with claws' – and she sets about nursing her back to health. She quickly sees that her husband's love for Shug makes him weak and vulnerable. He also reveals that Shug herself has no one else to turn to in her hour of need: 'Nobody fight for Shug', Albert says. She, too, needs a friend.[23]

It doesn't take long for Celie to fall in love with Shug. She cooks for her, bathes her, cuts her hair and makes dresses for her. For the first time she even feels she has something in common with her abusive husband, who wanted to marry Shug but was prevented from doing so by his father. The love she couldn't lavish on her children finds its object in Shug and soon they are unlikely but intimate friends. They briefly become lovers. And at last Celie's affection is rewarded: Shug orders Albert to stop beating her and to allow her out to his son's juke joint to hear Shug sing, and she is also instrumental in discovering where Albert has hidden all of Nettie's letters over the years.

Over the course of the novel, by confiding in her, Celie enables Shug to see the true extent of male brutality and power: 'You have to git man off your eyeball, before you can see anything a'tall', she finally admits.[24] Shug shows Celie that it is possible for a successful woman to be driven by ambition and sexuality: 'That when I notice how Shug talk and act sometimes like a man. Men says stuff like that to women, Girl, you look like a good time. Women always talk about hair and health.'[25]

The woman who looks like a 'good time' is Sofia, who is now married to Albert's son Harpo. Like Shug, she gets off to a bad start with Celie. They row when Sofia finds out Celie has given way to envy at Sofia's bravery and impulsively encouraged Harpo to beat her into submission. But Celie's remorse brings them together: 'I say it cause you do what I can't' (that is, stand up to your husband and punch him back), she confesses. Sofia asks her why she doesn't get angry. The exchange that follows epitomizes their different approach to life:

> This life soon be over, I say. Heaven last always.
>   You ought to bash Mr — head open, she say. Think bout heaven later.[26]

Both women find this hilarious, and from now on they are firm friends. Though Sofia undoubtedly shows Celie that it is possible to use anger to take control of your life, when she finds herself in jail for thumping the mayor she knows her only way to survive is to mimic Celie's meekness:

'Every time they ast me to do something, Miss Celie, I act like I'm you. I jump right up and do just what they say.'[27]

Sofia and her five big 'Amazon' sisters have grown up fighting their six brothers and watching their mother suffer under the tyranny of their father. She is naturally brave and surrounded by female support, a stark contrast to Celie's isolation and fear of Mr —. This means she can leave Harpo and stay with a sister instead. But her fierce temper both protects her – in domestic life – and ruins her, in that she doesn't stop to think of the consequences of punching a white man in authority. In the end it is Celie who has the nursing skills to bring Sofia back to health following a beating in prison, and who helps persuade her family to get her out of jail and into the position of maid at the mayor's house before she loses her temper again.

Celie's skills as a seamstress slowly come to the fore as the novel progresses. She makes curtains for Sofia and creates a quilt with her. Later, Shug donates some material for the quilt (a pattern called Sister's Choice) and sews a square herself: a symbol of the three women's intertwined and supportive lives. Then Celie moves on to make dresses for Shug. Shug recognizes her friend's talent, and when Celie is finally so enraged with Mr — (for not letting her see the letters from her sister Nettie) that she is behaving uncharacteristically like Sofia and close to slitting his throat Shug distracts her by setting up a tailoring project: 'every day we going to read Nettie's letters and sew'.[28]

This quiet, domestic chore is what liberates Celie, just as her ability to nurture has won her the loyalty and support of two strong women. It gives her purpose once she has finally left Mr — and moved to Memphis with Shug. Her signature tailored trousers are what she can sell when, at the end of the novel, she inherits a house and store from her stepfather.

Celie's moment of self-realization comes during dinner at Sofia's sister's house, when she at last finds a voice with which to confront Mr — about hiding Nettie's letters and forcing her to work for him and his children. When she announces she is leaving with Shug he is slow on the uptake: 'What will people say, you running off to Memphis like you don't have a house to look after?' Shug's husband Grady chips in with: 'A woman cant git a man if peoples talk', and this statement is so ludicrously irrelevant now to each of the three friends that they laugh and laugh and say 'um *hum*', and slap the dinner table, and wipe tears of mirth from their eyes.[29]

Albert slowly comes to realize the power of female friendship, and as his problematic marriage mellows after Celie has gained her independence he tells her how incomprehensible it was to him at first:

> 'When she was mean and nasty to you, I understood. But when I looked around and the two of you was always doing each other's hair, I start to worry.'[30]

By the end of the story, Shug is still vulnerable to falling in love with inappropriate men, and her career is coming to an end. Sofia is slowly integrating back into her family, after eleven and a half years of enforced employment as a maid. She also now works for Celie in her store. United in her later years with her sister and children, Celie, against all odds, and in no small part due to the influence of Shug and Sofia, has become the strongest of the three friends.

Undercover Allies

OFFRED & MOIRA

The Handmaid's Tale by Margaret Atwood

Offred recounts via flashback the political coup that led
to the establishment of Gilead, a totalitarian theocracy in
which women are ranked and controlled according to their
ability to give birth and everyone is under scrutiny from the
brutal secret police, known as the Eyes. Being one of the
few fertile women, Offred has been designated a 'Handmaid'
whose job is to give birth to a senior official's child. At first
it seems there is no way out of this reproductive slavery,
but slowly she picks up hints of an underground network of
resistance to the ruthless regime.

MARGARET ATWOOD made a rule for herself when writing this
novel: she would not put in any law, ritual or punishment which
had not already been used at some point in history, somewhere
in the world. Written up on a typewriter in Berlin and published
in 1985, the novel was shortlisted for the Booker Prize in 1986
(Atwood was joint winner of the prize for her follow-up book, *The
Testaments*, in 2019). In 2017 MGM/Hulu launched a hugely popular
television adaptation (in which Atwood played a cameo role), which

has continued in several series beyond the scope of the novel. In an example of the story seeping into everyday life, a motto Atwood uses from her schooldays – *nolite te bastardes carborundorum* (mock Latin for 'Don't let the bastards grind you down') – has become a popular tattoo among fans, and women around the world have adopted the red Handmaid's costume as a symbol of protest against attacks on women's rights.

OFFRED is thirty-three years old (the same age as Moira). She has brown hair and is an average height. There is nothing remarkable about her appearance, and once she has become a Handmaid she finds it difficult to recall what she used to look like. Offred is mourning the loss of her partner and daughter. She longs for an intimate relationship and feels empathy for everyone in her household, even her oppressors. Although in the original novel we never learn Offred's real name ('Offred' means 'of Fred'; that is, belonging to Fred Waterford, the Commander), fans have deduced that it could be June, since this name is whispered between the women when they are being re-educated at the Red Center. Although it wasn't her original intention, Atwood has said 'readers are welcome to it if they wish'.[31]

MOIRA wears her dark hair short and dresses unconventionally: purple dungarees, one fingernail painted gold, a single dangly earring. Athletic and emotionally brave – she speaks her mind without fearing the consequences – she also has stamina which enables her to stay on the run for longer than most (thanks also to the underground network of which she is part). Moira understands mechanics and is adept at improvising weapons and adopting disguises. She is always on the scrounge for cigarettes and can be single-minded and very persuasive: 'she's like a cat that crawls onto the page when you're trying to read.'[32]

T HE HANDMAID'S TALE is a feminist novel in that it powerfully and brilliantly exposes the cruelty and injustice of patriarchy. But it is not a one-dimensional allegory. Within the tale, women are as likely to betray people and enforce brutal laws as men are. The Aunts are older women whose specific job it is to re-educate fertile women in order to make them believe their sole function is to reproduce for their social superiors. Our heroine is no saint: she has had an affair with a married man; she is susceptible to mob mentality, despite her best intentions; she is suspicious of everyone in case they are spies for the regime. She decides not to 'risk' cultivating a friendship with Rita, the cook. She confesses she cannot pretend to like Serena Joy, the Commander's wife: 'I wanted to think I would have liked her, in another time and place, another life. But I could see already that I wouldn't have liked her, nor she me.'[33] Initially, she cannot get beyond formal exchanges with fellow Handmaid Ofglen, because they are mutually suspicious: 'she is my spy, as I am hers'.[34]

Trapped in her small room in the Commander's household, however, it is the memory of her best friend Moira that sustains Offred in her isolation and contrasts so strongly with the impossibility of finding friendships in Gilead. Alone at night she indulges in memories of how Moira would interrupt her studies and take her to the pub, how she would scrounge money and cigarettes and get away with it, how they would throw waterbombs at male students from their dorm window, how they would host outrageous student parties for a laugh. In later years they are close enough to disagree about many things – including the morality of Offred's affair with Luke compared to Moira's affairs with women – without affecting their bond: 'We could fight and wrangle and name-call, but it didn't change anything underneath. She was still my oldest friend.'[35] Disagreements in Gilead, by contrast, usually end in punishment or execution.

As the narrative progresses, and we learn more about Moira's life after the coup, she also becomes the friend who represents freedom, or the fantasy of it. At the Red Center, where the women are initially taken to be 'trained' for their role as Handmaids, Moira turns up just in time to remind Offred of life before the coup. It is four days before they can speak freely – 'friendships were suspicious' – through a hole in the partition between two toilet cubicles. Offred is ecstatic at having her friend with her. But after Moira's first failed attempt at escape she confesses: 'she made us dizzy. Already we were losing the taste for freedom, already we were finding these walls secure.' It is enough, at this point, for Offred to be in proximity to her friend, to be able to touch her fingers through the hole in the wall, to 'feel safer' with Moira there. But, conversely, the reassurance is due to the fact that Moira absolutely refuses to be brainwashed. Always outspoken, her first words to Offred are 'This is a loony bin.'[36] After Moira's second – and successful – escape attempt (having survived the brutal punishment for her first effort), she becomes a talisman: 'Moira was our fantasy. We hugged her to us, she was with us in secret, a giggle; she was lava beneath the crust of daily life.'[37]

As a narrator, Offred admits that she reconstructs, that she sometimes deviates from the facts. But when she learns what has happened to Moira since her escape from the Red Center, she tells her story as faithfully as she is able to: 'I've tried to make it sound as much like her as I can. It's a way of keeping her alive.'[38] By recounting the story (spoken into cassette tapes disguised as random music recordings, it later emerges), Offred is willing her friend to prevail. Earlier she explains that a story is similar to a letter: '*Dear You*, I'll say.... I will say *you, you*, like an old love song. *You* can mean more than one.'[39] Among the plural 'you' are Offred's missing daughter, mother, partner and, of course, her best friend.

In their last encounter in the book, Moira is in forced prostitution at Jezebel's club and the two friends are reunited when Offred is brought there in secret by her Commander, on an illegal night out. As usual, Moira is far more knowledgeable about the regime than Offred and explains that many of the commanders behave like this. She is still the more practical of the two friends, telling Offred not to cry because it will waste precious time. But she has also become resigned to her fate, in a way that alarms Offred: she jokes about the advantages of having access to drink and drugs, she describes the club as a 'Butch paradise'. What Offred hears in her voice, however, is defeatism, and this scares her more than anything:

> 'I don't want her to be like me. Give in, go along, save her skin... I want gallantry from her, swashbuckling, heroism, single-handed combat. Something I lack.'[40]

This last meeting puts into focus the differences between the two friends and, on a broader level, the contrasting reactions to the regime: resist or submit, the outcome is pretty much the same for both.

Even so, Offred gives us some alternative reconstructions of the next stage of her friend's life, showing how Moira lives on in her imagination, and allowing us as readers to pick our own ending:

> 'I'd like to tell a story about how Moira escaped, for good this time. Or if I couldn't tell that, I'd like to say she blew up Jezebel's, with fifty Commanders inside it. I'd like her to end with something daring and spectacular, some outrage, something that would befit her.'[41]

But, totally in keeping with the all-powerful regime of Gilead, Offred has no certainty about the fate of her friend. Perhaps this is partly why she retreats into a risky physical relationship with the chauffeur, Nick, instead of gathering information on the Commander for the resistance. She has seen how the regime has 'taken ... away something ... that used to be so central'; she has seen Moira's uninterested gaze, heard the 'lack of volition' in her voice.[42] Offred becomes reckless, mentioning Moira's real name to Nick, and when Ofglen, who turns out to be a secret member of the resistance, is taken away by the Eyes, she is terrified that the same thing will happen to her, and she will crack under interrogation and betray the friend she needs so much: 'Moira was right about me. I'll say anything they like, I'll incriminate anyone.'[43]

For Offred, life without intimacy, human touch, genuine friendship is not worth preserving. A bleaker narrative than the ones she suggests is clearly possible, just as at the end of the book, when the black van – which may or may not be part of the resistance – comes for her, Offred has no idea whether she is being taken 'into the darkness within; or else the light'.

'Are there any questions?' This is the bold, final line of the novel. Of course there are many, some of which are answered by *The Testaments*, although Moira doesn't feature in this second story, and Offred appears only at the very end. From the record of the symposium on Gileadean Studies in 2195, reproduced at the end of the novel, we know that Offred's tapes somehow reached England and are now the subject of academic study. In her small way she has succeeded in 'willing' her friend's continuing existence, albeit only in academic papers: 'I tell, therefore you are.'[44]

For Better, for Worse

ELENA & LINA

My Brilliant Friend, The Story of a New Name,
Those Who Leave and Those Who Stay &
The Story of the Lost Child by Elena Ferrante

Elena and Lina are growing up in a poor neighbourhood of
Naples in the economically depressed 1950s. The same age,
they both excel at school and are drawn to each other. But
while Elena's family grudgingly let her continue her studies
beyond the age of eleven, Lina's refuse to allow her to go up
to middle school. As their lives take different paths through
careers, marriage and motherhood, each achieves success
and suffers failure in different ways, always coming back to
the bond they formed in the tenement courtyard aged six.
Their stories take the measure of both personal and political
progress as Italy goes through the turbulent changes of the
second half of the twentieth century.

The Neapolitan novels were published in Italy between 2011 and 2014.
ELENA FERRANTE wrote Lina and Elena's story as a continuous
narrative, and then divided it into four books. The series has since
been translated into many languages. In a story that is so concerned
with identity – changing it, surrendering to it, destroying it – it is apt
that there is controversy even over the identity of the author. Elena

Ferrante is a pseudonym; though several claim to have discovered the real-life writer behind the name, others have condemned their investigations, arguing, as the author has done, that the books stand in their own right and if their author chooses to be anonymous we should all respect that choice.

ELENA GRECO is the daughter of a porter at the city council. She is naturally studious, hard-working, competitive and determined to do well at school – accustomed to being top of the class until Lina comes along. Elena lacks confidence and searches for approval from her teachers as well as her friend. She is terrified of turning into her mother, who has a limp, a short temper and a squint. Studying is a way to escape from oppressive home life in a cramped apartment and the expectation that girls should marry young and have children. Elena is fair, voluptuous and pretty, though she goes through a difficult puberty. She has a compulsion to hide her true feelings. By the end of the series she has three grown-up daughters and several books to her name.

LINA (LILA) CERULLO is the daughter of the local shoemaker. As a young girl she is skinny, dirty and covered in bruises. Elena likens her to a salted anchovy. She has a long face and black hair (the contrast between this and Elena's fair complexion echoing back to the conventions in Scott's and Eliot's work; see p.110) and when she is angry her eyes narrow to slits. But when Lina hits puberty she becomes beautiful, adored by the men of the neighbourhood. Lina is a quick learner and an original thinker: she refuses to conform to society's patriarchal expectations and stands up to the dangerous Solara brothers. She is capable of great influence but she is also mean and sharp-tongued: 'We made a pact when we were children: I'm the wicked one', she tells Elena's professor.[45] Lina has a son and a daughter, who is tragically lost at the age of four.

THE NEAPOLITAN NOVELS are narrated by Elena in a sustained feat of gripping narrative that is really an extended portrait of her complex friendship with Lina over the course of fifty years. *My Brilliant Friend* opens in the present day, with Lina's disappearance, and then sweeps us back in time to their first encounter. Elena's motivation for writing all this down is, she says, to prevent Lina from vanishing, to preserve her through words. She refuses to allow Lina to disappear from the historical record (as so many women before her have done), and she won't let go of their friendship.

Elena's view of her friend, though, is subjective, jealous and contradictory, and this is what makes her narrative endlessly engrossing. It also reflects Lina's changing identities over the decades as she and Elena come up against the restrictions of a brutally patriarchal society. Elena even has her own pet name for Lina – 'Lila' – exclusive to her, which shows us we are getting Elena's intimate version of this exasperating and competitive relationship.

Elena pinpoints the moment at which their bond is properly formed when they are eight years old, setting the pattern for the relationship that follows. They have been playing together with their dolls in the courtyard, and the day they decide to swap, Lina, being mean, drops Elena's doll through the grating into the dark basement. Elena immediately does the same to Lina's doll. They cannot find them again and believe Don Achille has taken them, because he is at that time the most terrifying figure in the neighbourhood, with a suspiciously large black bag. Weeks later, wanting a resolution to the crisis she herself has engineered, Lina decides it is time to confront the ogre and get them back, and Elena, as usual, follows her:

> We climbed slowly toward the greatest of our terrors of that time, we went to expose ourselves to fear and interrogate it.
> At the fourth flight Lila did something unexpected. She stopped to wait for me, and when I reached her she gave me her hand. This gesture changed everything between us forever.[46]

The double bravery of the two girls in this episode – confronting the most powerful man they can imagine – is something they will need to draw on over and over again in the course of their lives.

Elena is often described as Lina's shadow and criticized for blindly doing whatever her friend does, but by following her she challenges herself and gains access to new territories, new experiences. She sees Lina instinctively as her means of escape from the neighbourhood (rather like young Meena's intoxication with Anita; see p. 38):

> Something convinced me then, that if I kept up with her, at her pace, my mother's limp, which had entered into my brain and wouldn't come out, would stop threatening me. I decided that I had to model myself on that girl, never let her out of my sight.[47]

Her instincts are right: instead of pulling a knife on them, which is what both girls expect, Don Achille gives them some money to buy new dolls. It is Lina's idea to spend this money on a book, and she chooses *Little Women*, a story they both adore. It sparks ambition in them: at the age of just ten Lina writes her own story in response to it, but Elena imagines a shared success, completing their studies together and writing books that will make them both rich. Already their friendship is changing her life, and their girlhood passion for both dolls and books foreshadows a time in the future when Elena will be a published writer and they will both be expecting a child.

When they are young, their joint enterprise is to change or leave the neighbourhood. At one point, Lina pretends a monster has murdered Don Achille (not the local carpenter whom he beat up and who has been imprisoned for the killing) and that the carpenter's daughter is in love with Don Achille's son. Elena understands her story immediately:

> We were twelve years old, but we walked along the hot
> streets of the neighborhood ... like two old ladies taking the
> measure of lives of disappointment, clinging tightly to each
> other. ... We together, we alone, knew how the pall that had
> weighed on the neighborhood forever ... might lift at least
> a little if Peluso, the former carpenter, had not plunged the
> knife into Don Achille's neck, if it was an inhabitant of the
> sewers who had done it.[48]

Perhaps this ambition is one of the elements that keeps their friendship intact even when they fall in love with the same man: Nino Sarratore. Elena is the first to receive a kiss from him just as she turns fifteen during her first short holiday on Ischia. When she returns to the island for another holiday with newly married Lina, however, Nino diverts his attentions to her more glamorous friend, who is equally attracted to him.

Elena never admits to Lina that she is still in love with Nino and suffers agonizing jealousy in silence, even while facilitating their clandestine meetings. Looking back, she questions why that should be. Perhaps she was afraid that knowing Elena was in love with Nino would not have changed Lina's behaviour in any way, and that would be difficult to forgive. Perhaps she saw that Nino offered Lina a temporary escape from a violent and miserable marriage and wanted this for her friend. Conversely, when, years later, Elena begins her own extramarital affair with Nino, Lina doesn't hold back, telling Elena that if she leaves her husband for Nino it will make her a terrible mother. At the end of the short-lived relationship, Lina bluntly tells her that Nino has been flirting with her again. Elena survives the split by finishing a second novel and moving into the flat above her friend's apartment.

Over the long term, despite the incredible pain it causes, Elena and Lina's friendship transcends their joint infatuation with Nino. Elena recognizes her feelings of jealousy and envy, but represses them because she knows how potentially destructive they are. Lina, for her part, admits 'I'm bad, I don't even know how to keep friendship alive… So please, … if I say ugly things to you, stop up your ears, I don't want to do it and yet I do.'[49]

For a while, Lina tries to keep up with Elena by studying what she studies. Her search for an identity of her own is reflected in the way her name changes (the second book is titled *The Story of a New Name*) and also through the 'out-of-body' experiences from which she suffers throughout her life, when she feels that the outline of her body is disappearing and she is literally merging with her environment, no longer distinguishable as a human being. At one point she deconstructs a photograph of herself in her wedding dress, removing her face. By contrast, Elena secretly feels that 'I would truly exist only at the moment when my signature, Elena Greco, appeared in print'.[50] And Elena does in fact achieve success as a writer. She admits, though, throughout the novels, that her best writing is inspired by Lina's ideas. The admission fills her with guilt and envy, but she knows that she will always have this debt to her friend: 'What I could become outside of Lina's shadow counted for nothing.'[51]

Through this portrait we see the debt owed to the subjects that influence or inspire us, by those (especially women) who leave to those who stay, and the way our backgrounds shape us. Lina – often cruel and manipulative – in turn draws satisfaction from pushing her friend to succeed by competing with her. Though Lina is the dazzling one, Elena is the 'brilliant friend' of the title. She is the heroine in Lina's version of her life, and Lina criticizes her sharply if at any point she looks like failing in her role. She needs Elena's attention even when her own self-destructiveness seems to reject it: 'Watch me, always, even when you leave Naples', she tells Elena. 'That way I'll know that you see me and I'm at peace.'[52]

Towards the end of the final book, Elena, now a consultant at a publishing company, invites Lina to write something. Always competitive, she is slightly relieved when nothing materializes. But this, together with her friend's absence, frees her to create (though Lina has expressly forbidden it) this mesmerizing, contradictory, forensically detailed and unforgettable portrait of her friend's harsh and inspirational life and the battles she lost and won:

> I loved Lila. I wanted her to last. But I wanted it to be I
> who made her last. I thought it was my task. I was convinced
> that she herself, as a girl, had assigned it to me.[53]

Notes

Introduction

1. See Christopher Morley, 'In Memoriam Sherlock Holmes', *The Penguin Complete Sherlock Holmes*, Penguin, Harmondsworth, 1981.
2. Oscar Wilde, *The Importance of Being Earnest*, 1899, Act 1.
3. Interview by Anita Sethi, *Guardian*, 8 February 2020.
4. *Being Bridget Jones*, documentary, BBC Two, December 2020.

Childhood

1. Juliet Barker, *The Brontës*, Weidenfeld & Nicolson, London, 1994, p. 135.
2. Charlotte Brontë, *Jane Eyre*, ch. 20.
3. Ibid., ch. 8.
4. Ibid., ch. 6.
5. Ibid., ch. 7.
6. Ibid., ch. 8.
7. Ibid., ch. 21.
8. Ibid., ch. 10.
9. Ibid., ch. 18.
10. Ibid., ch. 27.
11. Ibid., ch. 33.
12. Ernest Hemingway, *The Green Hills of Africa*, Jonathan Cape, London, 1936, p. 29.
13. Quoted in the *Guardian*, 5 January 2011.
14. Mark Twain, *The Adventures of Tom Sawyer*, American Publishing Company, Cincinnati, 1876, ch. 6.
15. Mark Twain, *The Adventures of Huckleberry Finn*, Charles L. Webster & Co., New York, 1885, ch. 3.
16. Twain, *The Adventures of Tom Sawyer*, ch. 35.
17. Ibid., ch. 6.
18. Ibid., ch. 17.
19. Ibid., ch. 35.
20. Twain, *The Adventures of Huckleberry Finn*, ch. 7.
21. Ibid., ch. 15.
22. Ibid., ch. 31.

23. Ibid., ch. 33.
24. See, for example, Leo Marx, 'Mr. Eliot, Mr. Trilling, and "Huckleberry Finn"', *The American Scholar*, vol. 22, no. 4, 1953, pp. 423–44.
25. Twain, *The Adventures of Huckleberry Finn*, ch. 38.
26. Ibid., ch. 43.
27. See, for example, Shelley Fisher Fishkin, *Was Huck Black?*, Oxford University Press, New York, 1993; Brook Thomas, 'Adventures of Huckleberry Finn and Reconstruction', *American Literary Realism*, vol. 50, no. 1, 2017, pp. 1–24.
28. Twain, *The Adventures of Tom Sawyer*, ch. 24.
29. Twain, *The Adventures of Huckleberry Finn*, ch. 43.
30. L.M. Montgomery, *Anne of Green Gables*, ch. 5.
31. L.M. Montgomery, *Anne of Avonlea*, ch. 26.
32. L.M. Montgomery, *Anne of the Island*, ch. 12.
33. Montgomery, *Anne of Green Gables*, ch. 8.
34. Ibid., ch. 12.
35. Ibid., ch. 21.
36. Ibid., ch. 17.
37. Montgomery, *Anne of Avonlea*, ch. 13.
38. Ibid., ch. 29.
39. Ibid., ch. 19.
40. Montgomery, *Anne of Green Gables*, ch. 36.
41. Montgomery, *Anne of the Island*, chs 28–29.
42. A.A. Milne, *The House at Pooh Corner*, Egmont, London, 2016, ch. 8.
43. A.A. Milne, *Winnie-the-Pooh*, Egmont, London, 2016, ch. 3.
44. Ibid., ch. 7.
45. Milne, *The House at Pooh Corner*, ch. 8.
46. Ibid., ch. 3.
47. Milne, *Winnie-the-Pooh*, ch. 9.
48. Meera Syal, *Anita and Me*, Flamingo, London, 1996, ch. 13.
49. E.M. Forster, *A Passage to India*, ch. 2.
50. Syal, *Anita and Me*, ch. 3.
51. Ibid., ch. 6.
52. Ibid.
53. Ibid., ch. 7.
54. Ibid., ch. 6.
55. Muriel Spark, *The Prime of Miss Jean Brodie*, Macmillan, London, 1961, ch. 2.
56. Syal, *Anita and Me*, ch. 8.
57. Ibid., ch. 12.
58. Zadie Smith, *White Teeth*, Penguin, London, 2000, p. 86.
59. www.scholastic.com/teachers/articles/teaching-content/jk-rowling-interview.
60. J.K. Rowling, *Harry Potter and the Deathly Hallows*, Bloomsbury, London, 2007, ch. 4.
61. J.K. Rowling, *Harry Potter and the Order of the Phoenix*, Bloomsbury, London, 2003, ch. 26.

62. J.K. Rowling, *Harry Potter and the Half-Blood Prince*, Bloomsbury, London, 2005, ch. 15.
63. Rowling, *Harry Potter and the Deathly Hallows*, ch. 16.
64. J.K. Rowling, *Harry Potter and the Chamber of Secrets*, Bloomsbury, London, 1998, ch. 14.
65. J.K. Rowling, *Harry Potter and the Philosopher's Stone*, Bloomsbury, London, 1997, ch. 16.
66. Rowling, *Harry Potter and the Deathly Hallows*, ch. 22.
67. Rowling, *Harry Potter and the Half-Blood Prince*, ch. 30.
68. Ibid., ch. 32.
69. Rowling, *Harry Potter and the Deathly Hallows*, ch. 34.

Students and Apprentices

1. William Shakespeare, *Hamlet*, 1.1.68, in *The Oxford Shakespeare: The Complete Works*, 2nd edn, Oxford University Press, Oxford, 2005.
2. Ibid., 1.1.147–152.
3. Ibid., 1.2.174.
4. Ibid., 1.4.50–51.
5. Ibid., 1.5.166–169.
6. Ibid., 1.5.137; 5.1.201.
7. Ibid., 3.2.274–278.
8. Ibid., 4.6.23–24.
9. Ibid., 5.2.63–69.
10. Ibid., 5.2.166–170.
11. Ibid., 5.2.298–301.
12. Ibid., 5.2.312–313.
13. Ibid., 5.2.349; 5.2.333–339.
14. Charles Dickens, *Great Expectations*, ch. 22
15. Ibid., ch. 21.
16. Ibid., ch. 22.
17. Ibid.
18. Ibid., ch. 36.
19. Ibid., ch. 41.
20. Ibid., ch. 58.
21. Barbara Cooke, *Evelyn Waugh's Oxford*, Bodleian Library Publishing, Oxford, 2018, p. 46.
22. Evelyn Waugh, *Brideshead Revisited*, Penguin, London, 2000, bk 1, ch. 1.
23. Ibid., bk 1, ch. 2.
24. Ibid., Epilogue.
25. Ibid., bk 1, ch. 1.
26. Ibid., bk 1, ch. 4.
27. Ibid., bk 1, ch. 4.
28. Ibid.
29. Ibid., bk 1, ch. 5.
30. Ibid.
31. Ibid., bk 11, ch. 1.

32. Ibid., bk 2, ch. 1
33. Ibid.
34. Ibid., bk 3, ch. 1.
35. Ibid., bk 3, ch. 4.
36. Alan Taylor, 'The Prime of Miss Kay', *Times Literary Supplement*, 13 October 2017.
37. Muriel Spark, *The Prime of Miss Jean Brodie*, Macmillan, London, 1961, ch. 4.
38. Ibid., ch. 5.
39. Ibid., ch. 1.
40. Ibid.
41. Ibid., ch. 6.
42. Ibid., ch. 2.
43. Ibid., ch. 4.
44. Ibid., ch. 1.
45. Ibid., ch. 6..
46. Ibid.
47. Ibid., ch. 4.
48. Hannah Rosefield, 'The Cult of Donna Tartt', *Prospect*, 12 February 2013.
49. Donna Tartt, *The Secret History*, Little, Brown, London, 1992, ch. 5.
50. Ibid., ch. 1.
51. Ibid.
52. Ibid., ch. 2.
53. Ibid., ch. 5.
54. Ibid., ch. 8.
55. Ibid.
56. Ibid., Epilogue.
57. Ibid., ch. 8.

Heart to Heart

1. The First Folio is the first collected edition of Shakespeare's plays, published posthumously in 1623. There are two copies of the First Folio in the Bodleian Library.
2. James Shapiro, *1599: A Year in the Life of William Shakespeare*, Faber, London, 2011, p. 127.
3. William Shakespeare, *As You Like It*, 2.7.139–166, in *The Oxford Shakespeare: The Complete Works*, 2nd edn, Oxford University Press, Oxford, 2005.
4. Ibid., 1.1.103–107.
5. Ibid., 1.2.18–19.
6. Ibid., 1.3.25–33.
7. Ibid., 1.2.243–244.
8. Ibid., 1.3.72–75.
9. The swans were traditionally associated with Venus, though Shakespeare here links them with Juno, goddess of marriage.
10. Ibid., 1.3.80–81.
11. Ibid., 1.3.90–104.

12. Ibid., 1.3.136–137.
13. Ibid., 3.2.175–176.
14. Ibid., 3.2.214–219.
15. Ibid., 3.2.239.
16. Ibid., 3.4.1–3.
17. Ibid., 3.4.36–38.
18. Ibid., 4.1.62–63.
19. Ibid., 4.1.191–192.
20. J.E. Austen-Leigh, *A Memoir of Jane Austen and Other Family Recollections* (1870), ed. Kathryn Sutherland, Oxford University Press, Oxford, 2002.
21. Jane Austen, *Emma*, vol. 1, ch. 1; ch. 5.
22. Ibid., vol. 2, ch. 2.
23. Ibid.
24. Ibid., vol. 1, ch. 1.
25. Ibid., vol. 2, ch. 2.
26. Ibid., vol. 2, ch. 6.
27. Ibid., vol. 3, ch. 6.
28. Ibid., vol. 3, ch. 12.
29. Ibid., vol. 3, ch. 16.
30. William Austen-Leigh and Richard Arthur Austen-Leigh, *Jane Austen, Her Life and Letters*, Smith, Elder, & Co., London, 1913, p. 307.
31. George Eliot, *The Mill on the Floss*, bk 1, ch. 2.
32. Ibid., bk 5, ch. 1.
33. Ibid., bk 6, ch. 10.
34. Ibid., bk 6, ch. 6.
35. Ibid., bk 1, ch. 7.
36. Ibid., bk 6, ch. 2.
37. Ibid., bk 6, ch. 6.
38. Ibid., bk 6, ch. 7.
39. Ibid., bk 6, ch. 13.
40. Ibid., bk 7, ch. 3.
41. Ibid., bk 6, ch. 7.
42. Ibid.
43. Ibid., bk 6, ch. 2.
44. Ibid., bk 7, ch. 4.
45. Ibid.
46. *Being Bridget Jones*, documentary, BBC Two, December 2020.
47. 'Bridget Jones's Diary by Helen Fielding', *Bookclub*, BBC Radio 4, 3 November 2019.
48. Helen Fielding, *Bridget Jones's Diary*, Picador, London, 1996, p. 27.
49. Helen Fielding, *Bridget Jones: The Edge of Reason*, Picador, London, 1999, p. 194.
50. Fielding, *Bridget Jones's Diary*, p. 59.
51. Ibid., p. 21.
52. Ibid., p. 76.
53. Ibid., p. 37.
54. Ibid., p. 265.

55. Ibid., p. 271.
56. Fielding, *Bridget Jones: The Edge of Reason*, p. 21.
57. Fielding, *Bridget Jones's Diary*, p. 289.
58. Ibid., p. 42.
59. Ibid., p. 265.
60. Fielding, *Bridget Jones: The Edge of Reason*, p. 402.

Adventure

1. Miguel de Cervantes, *Don Quixote*, trans. Edith Grossman, Harper-Collins, London, 2004, pt II, ch. LVIII.
2. See, for example, Harold Bloom's introduction to *Don Quixote*, trans. Edith Grossman, HarperCollins, London, 2004.
3. Cervantes, *Don Quixote*, pt I, ch. XXI.
4. Ibid., pt I, ch. XVIII.
5. Ibid., pt II, ch. X.
6. Ibid., pt II, ch. XXIII.
7. Ibid., pt II, ch. LIV.
8. Ibid.
9. Ibid., pt II, ch. IV.
10. *OED* definition.
11. Arthur Conan Doyle, *The Sign of Four*, ch. 3.
12. Arthur Conan Doyle, *The Hound of the Baskervilles*, ch. 12.
13. Arthur Conan Doyle, *A Study in Scarlet*, ch. 2.
14. Doyle, *The Hound of the Baskervilles*, ch. 14.
15. Arthur Conan Doyle, 'The Adventure of Silver Blaze', in *The Memoirs of Sherlock Holmes*.
16. Arthur Conan Doyle, 'A Scandal in Bohemia', ch. 2, in *The Adventures of Sherlock Holmes*.
17. Doyle, *The Hound of the Baskervilles*, ch. 10.
18. Ibid., ch. 1.
19. Doyle, 'A Scandal in Bohemia', ch.2.
20. Doyle, *A Study in Scarlet*, ch. 5.
21. Doyle, *The Hound of the Baskervilles*, ch. 5.
22. Arthur Conan Doyle, 'The Adventure of the Three Garridebs', in *The Case Book of Sherlock Holmes*.
23. Doyle, *The Sign of Four*, ch. 1.
24. Arthur Conan Doyle, 'The Adventure of the Empty House', in *The Return of Sherlock Holmes*.
25. Ibid.
26. Kenneth Grahame, *The Wind in the Willows*, Methuen, London, 1908, ch. 1.
27. Ibid.
28. Ibid., ch. 2.
29. Ibid., ch. 5.
30. Ibid.
31. Ibid., ch. 1.

32. Ibid., ch. 9.
33. Ibid.
34. See Peter Hunt, *The Making of the Wind in the Willows*, Bodleian Library Publishing, Oxford, 2018, p. 20.
35. Grahame, *The Wind in the Willows*, ch. 12.
36. J.R.R. Tolkien, letter to H. Cotton Minchin, 16 April 1956.
37. J.R.R. Tolkien, *The Lord of the Rings*, Part 1: *The Fellowship of the Ring*, bk 1, ch. 2.
38. Ibid., bk 11, ch. 5.
39. Catherine McIlwaine, *Tolkien: Maker of Middle-earth*, Bodleian Library Publishing, Oxford, 2018, pp. 94–5.
40. Tolkien, *The Fellowship of the Ring*, bk 1, ch. 2.
41. Ibid., bk 1, ch. 2.
42. Ibid., bk 1, ch. 4.
43. Ibid., bk 11, ch. 10.
44. J.R.R.Tolkien, *The Lord of the Rings*, Part 3: *The Return of the King*, bk vi, ch. 3.
45. Tolkien, *The Fellowship of the Ring*, bk 11, ch. 10.
46. Tolkien, *The Return of the King*, bk vi, ch. 3.
47. J.R.R. Tolkien, *The Lord of the Rings*, Part 2: *The Two Towers*, bk iv, ch. 10.
48. Ibid., ch. 5.
49. Ibid., ch. 8.
50. Tolkien, *The Return of the King*, bk vi, ch. 9.
51. Tolkien, *The Fellowship of the Ring*, bk 11, ch. 3.

Hard Times

1. See Susan Shillinglaw, Introduction to *Of Mice and Men*, Penguin, London, 1994.
2. John Steinbeck, *Of Mice and Men*, Penguin, London, 2000, p. 2.
3. Ibid.
4. Ibid., p. 6.
5. Ibid., p. 13.
6. Ibid., p. 33.
7. Ibid.
8. Ibid., p. 112.
9. Ibid., p. 120.
10. Ibid., p. 8.
11. Ibid., p. 118.
12. Chinua Achebe, *Things Fall Apart*, Penguin, London, 2001, ch. 8.
13. Ibid., ch. 13.
14. Ibid., ch. 8.
15. Ibid., ch. 13.
16. Ibid., ch. 20.
17. Ibid.
18. Ibid., ch. 24.
19. Ibid., ch. 25.

20. Alice Walker, *The Color Purple*, 25th anniversary edn, Orion, London, 1992, p. 34.
21. Ibid., p. 45.
22. Ibid., p. 1.
23. Ibid., pp. 46–8.
24. Ibid., p. 196.
25. Ibid., p. 81.
26. Ibid., pp. 40–42
27. Ibid., p. 88.
28. Ibid., p.147.
29. Ibid., p. 200.
30. Ibid., p. 270.
31. Margaret Atwood, *The Handmaid's Tale*, Vintage, London, 2017, Introduction.
32. Ibid., ch. 10.
33. Ibid., ch. 3.
34. Ibid., ch. 4.
35. Ibid., ch. 28.
36. Ibid., ch. 13.
37. Ibid., ch. 22.
38. Ibid., ch. 38.
39. Ibid., ch. 7.
40. Ibid., ch. 38
41. Ibid.
42. Ibid.
43. Ibid., ch. 44.
44. Ibid., ch. 41.
45. Elena Ferrante, *Those Who Leave and Those Who Stay*, Europa Editions, New York, 2014, ch. 37.
46. Elena Ferrante, *My Brilliant Friend*, Europa Editions, New York, 2012, bk I, ch. 1.
47. Ibid., bk I, ch. 7.
48. Ibid., bk II, ch. 6.
49. Ferrante, *The Story of the Lost Child*, Europa Editions, New York, 2015, bk I, ch. 52.
50. Ferrante, *My Brilliant Friend*, bk II, ch. 55.
51. Ferrante, *The Story of a New Name*, Europa Editions, New York, 2013, bk II, ch. 4.
52. Ferrante, *Those Who Leave and Those Who Stay*, ch. 46.
53. Ferrante, *The Story of the Lost Child*, bk II, ch. 51.

Further Reading

The Adventures of Huckleberry Finn

Coveney, P., Introduction to *The Adventures of Huckleberry Finn*, Penguin, London, 2003.

Fishkin, S., *Was Huck Black?*, Oxford University Press, New York, 1993.

Levy, A., *Huck Finn's America: Mark Twain and the Era that Shaped his Masterpiece*, Simon & Schuster, New York, 2015.

Shurin, J., 'The Adventures of Huckleberry Finn', in John Sutherland (ed.), *Literary Landscapes*, Modern Books, London, 2018.

Thomas, B. 'Adventures of Huckleberry Finn and Reconstruction', *American Literary Realism*, vol. 50, no. 1, Autumn 2017, pp. 1–24.

Anita and Me

Syal, M., 'Epigraph' to *Anita and Me*, HarperCollins, London, 1996.

Who Do You Think You Are?, BBC One, October 2004.

Anne of Green Gables

Epperly, E.R., *The Fragrance of Sweet-Grass: L.M. Montgomery's Heroines and the Pursuit of Romance*, University of Toronto Press, Toronto, 1993.

Paskin, W., 'The Other Side of Anne of Green Gables', *New York Times Magazine*, 27 April 2017.

As You Like It

MacGregor, N., *Shakespeare's Restless World*, Penguin, London, 2012.

Shapiro, J., *1599: A Year in the Life of William Shakespeare*, Faber, London, 2011.

Shakespeare, William, *The Oxford Shakespeare: The Complete Works*, 2nd edn, Oxford University Press, Oxford, 2005.

Shakespeare, William, *As You Like It*, ed. J. Dusinberre, Arden Shakespeare, Bloomsbury, London, 2006.

Smith, E., *The Making of Shakespeare's First Folio*, Bodleian Library Publishing, Oxford, 2015.

Smith, E., *This Is Shakespeare*, Pelican, London, 2019.

Whitfield, P., *Mapping Shakespeare's World*, Bodleian Library Publishing, Oxford, 2015.

Brideshead Revisited

Byrne, P., *Mad World: Evelyn Waugh and the Secrets of Brideshead*, Harper-Collins, London, 2009.

Cooke, B., *Evelyn Waugh's Oxford*, Bodleian Library Publishing, Oxford, 2018.

Hardyment, C., *Novel Houses*, Bodleian Library Publishing, Oxford, 2019.

Waugh, E., Preface, *Brideshead Revisited: The Sacred and Profane Memories of Charles Ryder*, Penguin, Harmondsworth, 1959.

Bridget Jones's Diary

Baker, S., 'Literary Landmarks: Bridget Jones's Diary', *Mslexia* 39, 2008.

Being Bridget Jones, documentary, BBC Two, December 2020.

'*Bridget Jones's Diary* by Helen Fielding', *Bookclub*, BBC Radio 4, 3 November 2019.

Carty-Williams, C., 'Let's Celebrate Bridget Jones Turning 25 – and Be Critical of Her, Too', *Guardian*, 15 August 2016.

Fielding, H., Comment in *Independent*, 26 March 2016.

Sethi, A., Interview with Candice Carty-Williams, *Guardian*, 8 February 2020.

Thomas, S., 'The Great Chick Lit Conspiracy', *Independent*, 4 August 2002.

The Color Purple

Edemariam, Aida, 'Free Spirit', interview with Alice Walker, *Guardian*, 23 June 2007.

Walker, A., Introduction to *The Color Purple*, 25th anniversary edn, Orion, London, 1992.

Don Quixote

Bloom, H., Introduction to *Don Quixote*, Penguin, London, 2003.

Cervantes, Miguel de, *Don Quixote*, trans. J. Ormsby, Smith, Elder & Co., London, 1885.

Cervantes, Miguel de, *Don Quixote*, trans. E. Grossman, Penguin, London, 2003.

Vaisey, D., *Bodleian Library Treasures*, Bodleian Library Publishing, Oxford, 2015.

Emma

Austen-Leigh, J.E., *A Memoir of Jane Austen and Other Family Recollections* (1870), ed. Kathryn Sutherland, Oxford University Press, Oxford, 2002.

Austen-Leigh. W., and Richard Arthur Austen-Leigh, *Jane Austen, Her Life and Letters*, Smith, Elder, and Co., London, 1913.

Byrne, P., *The Real Jane Austen: A Life in Small Things*, HarperCollins, London, 2013.

Davies, A. 'Austen's Horrible Heroine', *Telegraph*, 23 November 1996.

Mullan, J., *What Matters in Jane Austen*, Bloomsbury, London, 2012.

Sutherland, K. (ed.), *Jane Austen: Writer in the World*, Bodleian Library Publishing, Oxford, 2017.

Tomalin, C., *Jane Austen: A Life*, Viking, London, 1997.

Weldon, F., *Letters to Alice, on First Reading Jane Austen*, Michael Joseph, London, 1984.

Great Expectations

Ackroyd, P., Introduction to *Great Expectations*, Octopus, London, 1991.

Slater, M., *Charles Dickens*, Yale University Press, London, 2009.

Hamlet

Greenblatt, S., *Hamlet in Purgatory*, Princeton University Press, Princeton NJ, 2002.

Palfrey, S., and Emma Smith, *Shakespeare's Dead*, Bodleian Library Publishing, Oxford, 2016.

Shakespeare, William, *The Oxford Shakespeare: The Complete Works*, 2nd edn, Oxford University Press, Oxford, 2005.

Smith, E., *This Is Shakespeare*, Pelican, London, 2019.

The Handmaid's Tale

Atwood, M., Introduction to *The Handmaid's Tale*, Vintage, London, 2017.

Desta, Y., 'Margaret Atwood's *Handmaid's Tale* Sequel: Offred's Daughters Tell Their Stories', *Vanity Fair*, 4 September 2019.

Dockterman, E., 'Margaret Atwood and Elisabeth Moss on the Urgency of *The Handmaid's Tale*', *Time*, 12 April 2017.

Harry Potter

Berndt, K., and L. Steveker (eds), *Heroism in the Harry Potter Series*, Ashgate, Farnham, 2011.

Rowling, J.K., interview, *Scholastic*, 3 February 2000, www.scholastic.com/teachers/articles/teaching-content/jk-rowling-interview.

Jane Eyre

Barker, J., *The Brontës*, Weidenfeld & Nicolson, London, 1994.
Mullan, J., *How Novels Work*, Oxford University Press, Oxford, 2006.

The Mill on the Floss

Haight, G., *George Eliot: A Biography*, Oxford University Press, Oxford, 1968.
Hughes, K., 'Re-reading: George Eliot's *Mill on the Floss*', *Guardian*, 27 March 2010.
Uglow, J., *George Eliot*, Virago, London, 2008.

The Lord of the Rings

Carpenter, H., *J.R.R. Tolkien: A Biography*, George Allen & Unwin, London, 1977.
Garth, J., 'Sam Gamgee and Tolkien's Batmen', blog post, 13 February 2014, https://johngarth.wordpress.com/2014/02/13/sam-gamgee-and-tolkiens-batmen.
McIlwaine, C., *Tolkien: Maker of Middle-earth*, Bodleian Library Publishing, Oxford, 2018.
Tolkien, J.R.R., Foreword to *The Lord of the Rings*, 2nd edn, HarperCollins, London 2005.

My Brilliant Friend

Ferrante, Elena, interviewed by D. Jacob, *Los Angeles Times*, 17 May 2018.
Rainsford, S., 'A New Skin', in the National Theatre Official Programme for *My Brilliant Friend*, adapted by April de Angelis, 2020.

Of Mice and Men

Shillinglaw, S., Introduction to *Of Mice and Men*, Penguin, London, 1994.

The Prime of Miss Jean Brodie

McWilliam, C., Introduction to *The Prime of Miss Jean Brodie*, Penguin, London, 2000.
Taylor, A., 'The Prime of Miss Kay', *Times Literary Supplement*, 13 October 2017.

The Secret History

Kaplan, J., 'Introducing Donna Tartt', *Vanity Fair*, September 1999.
Rosefield, H., 'The Cult of Donna Tartt', *Prospect*, 12 February 2013.
Viner, K., 'A Talent to Tantalise', *Guardian*, 19 October 2002.

Sherlock Holmes

Morley, C., Introduction to Arthur Conan Doyle, *The Penguin Complete Sherlock Holmes*, Penguin, Harmondsworth, 1981.
Sutherland, J., 'Sherlock Holmes, the World's Most Famous Literary Detective', www.bl.uk, March 2014.
www.bakerstreetdozen.com/coca.html.
www.arthurconandoyle.com/biography.html.

Things Fall Apart

Bandele, B., Introduction to *Things Fall Apart*, Penguin, London, 2001.
Mpalive-Hangson, M., and David Whittaker, *Chinua Achebe's Things Fall Apart: A Routledge Study Guide*, Routledge, London, 2007.
Murad, M. 'Things Fall Apart', in John Sutherland (ed.), *Literary Landscapes*, Modern Books, London, 2018.

The Wind in the Willows

Harydment, C., *Writing the Thames*, Bodleian Library Publishing, Oxford, 2016.
Hunt, P., Introduction to *The Wind in the Willows*, Oxford University Press, Oxford, 1999.
Hunt, P., *The Making of the Wind in the Willows*, Bodleian Library Publishing, Oxford, 2018.

Winnie-the-Pooh

Brandreth, G., 'I knew Christopher Robin – the Real Christopher Robin', *Telegraph*, 19 October 1998.

Acknowledgements

I would like to thank all my friends at Bodleian Library Publishing for their invaluable support and creative ideas for this book: Samuel Fanous, Deborah Susman, Leanda Shrimpton, Susie Foster, Dot Little, Su Wheeler and Wendy Dashwood. I am grateful, too, for the advice and guidance of the Bodleian Library's Editorial Committee, and for that of Dr Helen Moore, Dr Barbara Cooke and the expert reader, all of whose feedback greatly enhanced the second draft, and to Lucy Morton and Robin Gable for all their editorial and design work.

A number of friends generously contributed brilliant ideas and suggestions to this project, but I am particularly indebted to Fiona Harvey, Anna Scott-Brown, Claire Sussums and Sarah Waldram for their insights, corrections and suggestions. A big thank you to Martin and Imogen for patiently discussing this book with me over many lockdown lunches, and to my parents for first encouraging me to explore so many of the literary works within these pages.

Index